Programme and Project Management Library

Programme Management

Case Studies

LONDON: HMSO

Acknowledgements   The assistance of authors from various consultancies, under contract to CCTA, in producing these case studies is acknowledged. Annex A gives a profile of each of the consultancies involved.

For further information regarding CCTA products please contact:

CCTA Library
Rosebery Court
St Andrew's Business Park
Norwich
NR7 0HS
01 603 704704

Contents

1 Introduction

1.1 Purpose

In today's public services, change is happening more rapidly and with greater impact than ever before. Initiatives such as Next Steps, the Citizen's Charter and market testing have changed the way public services are delivered. There is a drive towards improved choice, flexibility and value for money, and a need to provide better information to citizens on services available to them. Information needs arise from such initiatives, and are also identified in strategic planning of information systems (IS). IS strategies identify the portfolio of projects, policies and service requirements to support an organisation's changing business objectives.

The response to the challenges that face the public sector has to be managed effectively since it may involve daunting, large-scale changes to work patterns, information systems, organisation structures and ways of delivering services. Such changes must be introduced while the organisation's overall aims and objectives are kept in sight, and services to the public continue to operate without deterioration.

Programme management is the approach being adopted by a growing number of both the larger and the smaller public service organisations to manage this response, and to implement the portfolio of projects from IS strategies that support changing business objectives.

The case studies in this volume present early experience of programme management in government and other public sector organisations (or private organisations that impact on a wide public). The case studies are published in response to advice which has been sought by public sector organisations from CCTA: how to implement IS strategies involving significant change while maintaining the continuity of business operations. Government departments and agencies value insights into how other organisations have coped with problems similar to their own and seek confirmation that the approach they adopt has been successfully used elsewhere. These case studies offer such confirmation.

The case studies are based on presentations given at CCTA's Programme Management Conference held in December 1993 (London). They reflect the experience of large government departments and others, assisted by management consultancies, in identifying and setting up programmes.

The case studies have been written by members of the management consultancies who advised and assisted their client organisations in setting up programmes, and are presented, anonymously, from the point of view of the client organisations. Each case study concentrates on a particular aspect of programme management, with the common theme of the scale of change embarked upon across the organisations concerned.

The programmes described here were started before the publication of CCTA's guidance in this area, consequently they contain some differences in approach and terminology to that found in CCTA's other programme management publications. Throughout this volume the terms used are related to their equivalent or closely comparable usage in the CCTA recommended approach, and some explanation is given for variations in approach. Since customer organisations will need to adapt the best practice in the CCTA guidance to their own circumstances, such variation, in practice, does not detract from CCTA's recommendations.

1.2   Audience

Advisors to Chief Executives and senior business managers will read these case studies to confirm that programme management is a successful approach that can be applied to their own organisations. The case study *Scoping the programme* (Chapter 5) will provide insights into how getting the scoping right involves looking at the objectives being served. The final case study, *Changes in the programme* (Chapter 8), is convincing evidence that programme management is a resilient approach that can cope with changes in scope or direction forced by external pressures and new initiatives.

Top management may expect to appoint Programme Directors to lead the programmes that they set up. The case study on using a *blueprint* to define and describe future business operations (*Using a blueprint*, Chapter 6) and that on the Programme Director's role in managing the client/contractor relationship (*The role of the Programme Director*, Chapter 7) will be of interest.

IT Directors involved in the management of programmes and members of Programme Executives (fulfilling the roles of Programme Manager, Design Authority and Business Change Manager) will find *Mobilising a strategic IT programme in the public sector* (Chapter 3) a source of insight into these roles. *Managing change in the working environment* (Chapter 4) covers topics of special interest to Business Change Managers.

1.3   Structure of this volume

Chapter 2 describes how the case studies have been assembled and relates their themes to published CCTA guidance on programme management.

Chapters 3 to 8 contain the six case studies. Each case study is followed by a brief commentary from CCTA relating the specific issues raised in the case history to CCTA guidance (pointing out differences in approach where appropriate).

Annex A gives a short profile of the consultancies involved in the programmes, who provided the content of the case studies. They are listed in the order of the case study they were concerned with. These and other companies can provide third party support in setting up and running programmes, and training in programme management. Annex A does **not** constitute an 'approved' list of service providers.

A Bibliography gives further reading on programme management and the CCTA project management method PRINCE.

Finally there is a Glossary of the programme management and PRINCE terms found in the case studies. (For a more extensive set of definitions covering all programme management concepts, the reader is referred to CCTA's: *A Guide to Programme Management*, and for PRINCE definitions to the *PRINCE Reference Manuals*.)

2   Overview of the case studies

This volume presents a set of six case studies that will be of particular interest to organisations starting programme management for the first time, or adapting their existing practices towards the approach given in CCTA guidance on this topic.

The case studies have been chosen to illustrate how the contributors tackled key aspects of the approach in a practical way. The aspects focused on are:

- mobilising for programme management

- structuring the programme for effective management of change in the working environment

- scoping the programme

- the need for a vision of how the future business will operate (the *blueprint*), defining what the programme is trying to achieve

- the Programme Director's role

- coping with change to the programme's scope.

It is intended to follow up this volume with further case studies, offering practical illustration of topics such as managing business benefits from a programme, managing risks to the programme, programme quality and change control, and the transition from existing systems and processes into the new ways of working, arising from the programme's projects.

2.1   Fit with CCTA guidance

The views expressed in these case studies are from those involved in the programmes described, and do not necessarily represent an approach endorsed by CCTA.

All the programmes had been in progress some time before CCTA's guidance was published (and indeed influenced the putting together of the recommended approach), so a complete match to the concepts in CCTA's guidance will not be found. Where appropriate, there is discussion in the case study and in a summary from CCTA at the end of each reflecting on variations of approach.

2.2 Synopses

Mobilising a strategic IT programme in the public sector (Chapter 3)

This case study deals with getting programme management started in a large public sector organisation. Almost inevitably, it was not a 'green field' situation: some projects arising from the existing IS/IT Strategy were already underway when the programme started and there was a stable project management culture under the controlling influence of a 'projects branch'. This case study shows that a progressive approach to introducing programme management culture can produce benefits and be 'sold' to those used to managing separate projects. Programme management roles (Programme Manager, Design Authority and Business Change Manager) were adapted and where necessary added to.

Managing change in the working environment (Chapter 4)

Here a programme management organisation was set up to manage a programme of change, during which a large organisation was restructured into business units with devolved authority, and charged with becoming more customer-facing.

Scoping the programme (Chapter 5)

How is the programme scoped? By concentrating on benefits delivery, by alignment to business units (and nominating an individual within the business unit to be accountable for delivery of each benefit) the scope was kept within achievable bounds. Strong management of risk also helped to avoid the tendency for requirements to grow beyond what was affordable and achievable.

Using a blueprint (Chapter 6)

Set in a financial services environment, this case study shows how the blueprint was used to guide a change programme towards its objectives: as a vision of the future, as a communications vehicle which won hearts and minds in the organisation, as an aid to identifying and choosing options during programme definition, as a yardstick of achievement against the vision, and to help assess the impact of a shift in the programme's objectives.

The role of the Programme Director (Chapter 7)

Concentrating on the responsibilities of the Programme Director in a technically complex and safety-critical programme, this case study shows how to achieve an appropriate relationship and effective communication with a prime supplier, which helps in the management of costs and risk.

Changes in the programme (Chapter 8)

A short case study showing that programme management enables an organisation to deal successfully with change to its business objectives and to harness advances in technology while undertaking a major overhaul of its core business systems.

2.3 CCTA commentaries

At the end of each case study there is a brief commentary from CCTA. The commentary points to areas where the approach taken in the programme described differs from the best practice recommended by the Programme and Project Management Library publications on this topic. Since these programmes were underway while the CCTA guidance was being formulated, there are inevitably differences in terminology and practice. The CCTA commentary will enable the reader to understand these points of difference in terminology, structure or organisation without extensive cross-reference to the published guidance.

Glossary

To help the reader further, the glossary at the end of this volume gives CCTA's published definitions of those of its programme management terms to be found in these case studies, even if their usage in the case studies does not always exactly match CCTA's definition.

3 Mobilising a strategic IT programme in the public sector

This case study was provided by
PA Consulting

14

3   Mobilising a strategic IT programme in the public sector

3.1   Introduction

This is a case study about a government computer department supplying IT services to a large government organisation, which is charged with the implementation of a major IS/IT Strategy over a 10 year time span whilst continuing to operate two mainframe legacy systems all within a state of organisational 'turbulence' and funding shortage. The Strategy identified some 19 major IT projects to be developed over the next 10 years and a recent reorganisation is expected to increase this total to 30 projects in all. The approach to the case study is written with two main themes in mind:

> Programme management implementation was based on CCTA's now published guidance. In practice, the implementation of the organisation's Strategy had been running for some time and so it was necessary to run the first two CCTA phases, programme identification and programme definition, in parallel and '...jump on the bus after it had left the bus stop'.

> The approach was also based on the practical experience of many similar programme management assignments provided by the lead consultancy. The consultancy provided just a single, very experienced, consultant to introduce and set up programme management, to carry out the work of the Programme Manager and simultaneously to transfer skills to the civil servants nominated to take over on completion of the assignment.

The case study covers the first 12 months of the setting up and operation of programme management in the department. It is written from the viewpoint of the organisation's Programme Manager. Unlike project management, programme management is an ongoing management discipline that is planned to be further developed and refined over the 10 year life of the Strategy in this organisation.

3.2 The situation we were in

The main task of the department was to manage a large programme of work with the following attributes:

- ten year timeframe

- two major legacy systems

- multiple development and infrastructural projects

- staff numbers totalling 230 of which some 70 per cent were committed to the legacy systems

- Strategy implementation in 250 sites

- costs of £100m generating projected benefits of £200m.

The implementation of the programme needed to realise the Strategy was made more difficult by a 'turbulent' environment featuring:

- a new organisation

- many new business processes

- market testing

- changing and conflicting business priorities

- joint venture initiatives with other departments in the organisation

- restricted and uncertain funding.

By the end of 1992, the 10 year Strategy had been in place for almost two years. Multiple projects had been set up without any corporate co-ordination or control mechanisms. The line management approach through the 'Projects Branch' was not working well enough and the PRINCE projects were operating individually leading to both duplication of work plus 'cracks' where nothing was happening. There was a lack of short or long term focus and a wide, and growing, gulf between the Strategy and what was actually happening on the projects.

By this time, the department was also faced with the fact that the implementation of the organisation's Strategy was losing focus amidst a sea of organisational upheaval and 'turbulence', brought on by both dramatic role changes and projected severe funding restrictions. We had to continue with the implementation of the Strategy, but everything seemed against us. By the end of 1992, the Strategy had just been updated and consolidated. Several of the constituent projects had already been launched under conventional PRINCE guidelines and it was becoming clear that the individual projects and the Strategy were uncoordinated and beginning to diverge.

There were many organisational issues to be addressed, some of which were:

- how were we to maintain the link between the Strategy and the implementation of the individual projects?

- the 'Strategy Update' mechanism for updating the corporate plan at 12 to 18 monthly intervals was cumbersome. It could not keep up with the necessary changes that had to be incorporated for the individual PRINCE projects and Strategy to keep 'in synchronisation'

- the line management mechanism (the 'Projects Branch'), installed to try and keep the projects co-ordinated, was focused only on the short term problems of the PRINCE Stages currently running instead of the whole portfolio of projects. There was much uncoordinated work going on and, in particular, interdependencies between projects were a source of continuing problems

- there was no co-ordinated approach to the management of either the portfolio of projects or the supporting business model (which specified projected costs and benefits) on an ongoing basis.

Programme management appeared to offer the solution and, after open competition for expert consultancy support, programme management was formally launched in the department in February 1993.

3.3 How programme management was introduced

With several projects already running, the approach was based on the need to bring that work under the centralised supervision of programme management. In parallel, the Strategy documents were consolidated and updated to form the foundation for the portfolio of projects and a business model was produced to be able to validate the Strategy's business case. At that time, the ability to respond to impact statements was tested to the limit by no less than three succeeding budget reduction exercises resulting from the well publicised 'economy measures' affecting all Public Sector finances.

The CCTA guidance recommends that the four phases of programme management are:

1 Programme Identification
2 Programme Definition
3 Programme Execution
4 Benefits Realisation.

It was clear that with the initial Strategy projects already running there was to be no 'green field' start and so the two initial phases in the CCTA guidance, programme identification and programme definition, were therefore run in parallel with existing management activities, 'cutting over' to programme management procedures on a progressive basis.

The inexperience of the department, and the turbulent environment in which it was operating, meant that a patient and progressive approach was needed to establish the many new concepts of programme management and ensure a clear understanding of the differences from the management of individual projects under PRINCE and the department's hierarchical line management.

The actual approach adopted, was to introduce programme management progressively as a series of steps, at a pace that could be absorbed by the department's staff. The steps were:

- start with defining the Programme Plan

- prioritise the programme by bringing the high pay-back projects forward (catalysed by a 40 per cent cut in budget for the 1993/94 financial year!)

- refine the business model to suit. This costed the whole programme over the 10 year period and identified the cost savings over the same period

- set up the monthly progress and planning reporting cycle

- develop and produce a definitive, single, high-level programme progress report

- create the Programme Management Plan to document programme management topics and progressively implement programme level procedures.

The Programme Management Plan contains much of what would now be incorporated in the Programme Definition Statement. In our case, the Programme Management Plan started before the CCTA guidance was available and it was decided to continue rather than re-write and re-issue what had already been achieved. In particular, the main elements of new business *blueprint* had already been incorporated in the original documentation describing the Strategy and therefore a summary was incorporated into the programme overview contained in the Programme Management Plan. Currently a separate *blueprint* is being drawn up as the basis of an update to the Strategy, following its review.

Whilst this process is still going on at the time of writing, the feedback has been extremely encouraging and, within a matter of weeks of its introduction, programme management was recognised as a valuable and essential discipline in the implementation of both the Strategy and the constituent projects.

3.4 Mobilising the programme

The approach was based directly on the CCTA guidance which has provided some considerable source of inspiration (and occasionally, perspiration). Its progressive introduction enabled the department to digest the 'culture change' whilst still maintaining the daily operation of the programme.

The approach centred on seven major activities described as follows.

Scoping the overall programme

Within the organisation, each department has considerable freedom in the structure and expenditure profile of its yearly funding. In the construction of the programme, the portfolio of projects was balanced along with the other support projects set up to establish the department's capability and the operation and maintenance of the two legacy systems. The basis for scoping was the need to bring forward the high payback projects and defer the remaining projects to later tranches and thus present a good business case for the first tranche. This was undertaken in the light of both restricted funding and limited availablility of experienced staff. In the event, it was possible to transfer some experienced staff from the legacy systems to the projects for their replacement thus reducing costs and risks to the programme from recruiting completely fresh staff from outside.

In Spring 1993 the first Programme Plan was published. This bridged the gap between the Strategy and the individual projects. For the first time project interdependencies were clearly identified and explicitly shown on the programme plan.

Setting programme objectives

With the overall programme stretching over 10 years it was essential to set some short term objectives to ensure that the 'highest return' projects could be prioritised and completed at the earliest point. At the same time the necessary infrastructure and support projects needed to achieve this were defined.

The next step was to define a tranched approach by advancing, deferring and re-structuring the portfolio of projects to create the first tranche. This is scheduled for completion in 1995 with its constituent projects delivering the bulk of the benefits of the Strategy and thus represents the first **island of stability** in the programme.

Gaining control of the programme

With the programme plan defined, a monthly reporting and control cycle was set up. The progress on each of the constituent projects was summarised in a regular progress report based on a standardised turn-around of information from project and line managers in accordance with a published reporting cycle. The monthly programme progress report has now been established as the **single statement of status of the entire programme**. This represents a very significant improvement when compared with the previous situation where each project reported individually to their own Project Board at different times in the month, each with different format and content and completely uncoordinated!

Once the mechanism for producing the progress report had 'bedded in', work started to progressively refine it and upgrade it with financial reports showing the forecast expenditure against programme budget, league tables showing the achievement of the key project milestones and products, and the formal reporting and follow-up of programme-significant issues and risks.

Complementary to the planning and progress monitoring of the programme is the setting up of programme level procedures to ensure that control is maintained. These procedures include issue and risk management, project initiation and close down, and programme level change control. The emphasis here has been to introduce the minimum of additional procedures that can be driven effectively by the department rather than producing procedures that will just be followed by rote or are otherwise abandoned shortly after implementation. (In most IT departments there are cupboards full of unused self-generated procedures!) These procedures, and programme level guidelines, are being progressively documented in the Programme Management Plan (PMP) which describes how the programme is managed and which matches the programme plan that describes what the programme consists of.

Setting up the Design Authority

With the individual projects being managed under PRINCE, technical assurance was provided under the conventional Technical Assurance Co-ordinator (TAC) and Senior Technical roles. Initially, this seemed to

Delivering the
Programme
Management Plan

provide suitable coverage for the Design Authority role as envisaged by the CCTA guidance. However, experience has shown that an over-arching 'technical co-ordination' role can provide the essential linking both between the individual projects, and across the span of the programme that is otherwise missing. In practice, the Design Authority has been set up in the Projects Branch as this provided the most suitable position in line management terms.

Principles and procedures were progressively documented in the Programme Management Plan, which was produced in modules that were individually reviewed by Senior Management. This Plan defines how the programme is managed and contains much useful reference material so that it approaches a 'single source of reference'. The main sections were:

- Director's statement giving authority to programme management

- programme technical overview

- organisation and communication

- principles of programme management

- issue management and change control procedures

- planning, resource and organisational breakdown structures

- procedure for adding and removing projects from the programme

- overall programme plan in the form of a logic-linked bar chart

- schedule management procedure covering progress monitoring and reporting

- programme-level budgeting and benefits management principles and procedures

- programme cost and resource management principles and procedures

- Programme Management Information System (PMIS)

- quality Management and the link to the department's quality management system.

The Programme Management Plan was progressively rolled out as a key component in the Quality Management System produced in accordance with BS5750.

Developing the MIS for Programme Management

A Programme Management Information System (PMIS) is being developed based on a relational database that holds all the programme plan, resource and cost information in a single bespoke system. Previously this information had been held on several separate PCs in five different types of application and the benefits of migrating to a single system were obvious. The use of the relational database is key, since the need to compare different sources of data and to produce responses to senior management 'what-if' enquiries is a significant part of programme management life. The ability to manipulate future scenarios, and hold historical data once a project in the programme has been completed, means that lessons learnt can be incorporated in future plans before the sands of time cover up how the problems of the day were resolved.

The main objective of the PMIS is to provide the single authoritative source of programme information. At its simplest, this is embodied in the overall programme plan reproduced as a large multi-colour bar chart on the Director's office wall. It is amazing how project managers take an interest in the programme level representation of their project once they realise that it is visible at management's highest level!

Realising the Benefits

A Business Change Manager was recently appointed and is currently tasked with assessing the benefits claimed for the Strategy as held in the business model. The next steps involve setting up benefits monitoring on a monthly basis and developing a benefits realisation plan that will be incorporated in the programme. This plan will be based on evaluating each project in the programme:

- on completion – to ensure that the benefits realisation tasks for the project are in place

- six months after completion – to measure the initial realisation of benefits

- eighteen months after completion – to measure the 'final' realisation of benefits now that the new system has become 'Business as Usual'.

The appointment of the Business Change Manager 'closes the loop' in that this post will catalyse the production of the new business *blueprint* and thus ensure that the organisation is both able to absorb the new IS and benefit from it in terms of increased effectiveness and efficiency.

3.5   Lessons learnt from practical experience

Whilst the CCTA guidance has been drawn up on the basis of both industry and public sector experience, it is inevitable that practice may differ to some extent from the guidance. In the case of our department, the introduction of programme management is by no means complete yet considerable benefits are already emerging.

The following points reflect some real life issues from our experience.

Programme versus line and project management

Initially, in the department, there was some suspicion that programme management represented just another layer of bureaucracy. With several projects already underway the incumbent project managers had to be individually briefed and confidence won. The introduction of programme management was therefore approached on a 'softly-softly' basis emphasising the benefits. This has been very successful. Similarly, the position of programme management *vis-à-vis* the department's line management required careful handling whilst terms of reference were being established.

As a result, the organisational reporting lines turned out to be slightly different from what was suggested in the

CCTA guidance. The main difference was that the programme manager held a strong monitoring and advisory role with the actual execution of the programme being the responsibility of the head of Projects branch.

The lesson learnt is that programme management cannot just be imposed by managerial edict. It needs to be 'sold' internally if it is to be both accepted and effective and implemented progressively if it is to last. There is a continual need to gain consensus and a diplomatic approach is essential if tenuous lines of authority are not to be over-stretched!

Who runs the projects in the programme?

It is emphasised that the responsibility for the day-to-day management of the PRINCE projects in the programme rests with the individual project managers and the PRINCE boards they report to. In our department, programme management has global responsibilities for the overall shape and size of the programme and not for the conduct of individual projects. Furthermore, the CCTA guidance does not stress the typically strong influence of conventional hierarchical line management that is a feature of the Public Sector.

Skills transfer to permanent staff is essential

It is essential to transfer skills to permanent staff due to the long life of the programme. However, in our department, as in many other organisations, staff are inexperienced and therefore the skills transfer is expected to be prolonged. There were no courses to attend and, at the start, only the CCTA guidance to refer to! Implementing the principles and procedures took far longer that one would expect due to the degree of culture shock involved throughout the department.

It should also be noted that there are very few skilled and experienced programme managers in the UK, but lots of project managers that think they are programme managers! This was apparent when the job of programme manager was competed for at the start. This is because any programme is likely to last several years and therefore the rate of accumulation of experience in programme management is correspondingly slower than for project management. Skills transfer has been recognised as one of the most important benefits from the use of experienced consultancy.

Don't expect perfection!

Whilst an individual project may be considered to be a success (or otherwise!), the situation with a programme is always 'varying shades of grey'. In every programme there may well be one brilliant success and one real failure – with the rest somewhere in between. There is no such thing as the perfect programme implementation and to attempt it is to risk danger of searching for the 'holy grail'. Programme management is all about creating an improved performance over what would have been achieved otherwise.

Experience has shown that when implementing programme management, the recommendations in the CCTA guidance need not be taken as mandatory but as good advice on best practice – and that implementation should develop at a pace suitable for the organisation. Our experience is that it is best to get just one or two processes going successfully – then build on that success. Don't try and put everything in place at once!

The Programme must support the re-engineering of the business in order to deliver the benefits of the Strategy and realise the *blueprint*

In our department, the programme was all about re-engineering the business, creating a 'sea-change' in culture and supporting an organisation-wide change programme. In our case, it is 'the IS department', that is catalysing the need for the organisation to re-engineer its business. If that business is not re-engineered then many of the benefits of the Strategy will not be realised. The aim of our department is now to ensure the production of the new business *blueprint* that can be synchronised with the next update to the Strategy. Ideally, we would have preferred to follow the sequence recommended in the CCTA guidance and produce the *blueprint* first.

The department is already planning the delivery of programme benefits. However, it must be remembered that the benefits of the products of the programme can only be delivered by the organisation and not by our department. All too often the IS department gets blamed for the failure of the business to realise the benefits of new systems.

Programme management and the Project Support Office (PSO)

Our experience has indicated that it is best for programme management to collect its own data for the programme plan and progress reports. Whilst the conventional PRINCE PSO could, in theory, provide all the required information, practice has indicated that programme management needs to set up its own data collection procedures with the PSO concentrating its, generally limited, resources at project level. Some of the reasons for this are:

- PRINCE projects concentrate on managing the current project stage. Programme management looks across the whole life cycle of each project

- programme management is concerned with the position on both future and historical projects, as defined in the Strategy over a 10-year time frame, in the programme. Only a proportion of the total projects had PRINCE Boards in place at any one time and consequently the majority of projects in the programme did not have PSO-sourced plans or progress data

- programme management reports on the status and progress of the portfolio of projects at a single point each month. Each project reports to its project board individually at a different time in the month

- the data that programme management requires is produced from a different viewpoint to that required by the individual PRINCE project board. Essentially it is 'upward and outward' whereas individual project reports tend to concentrate 'inward and downward'

- there is little, if any, guidance in PRINCE on how the PSO is to support programme management. Consequently the typical BAC or TAC is inexperienced in the requirements of programme management.

The programme reflects the workload of the department

In our case, the programme plan incorporates all projects, whether completed, in progress, or planned, and includes the operation of the current systems, the provision of ongoing support and the realisation of business benefits. The programme therefore maps directly on to the workload of the IT department, and the programme plan thus forms the basis of the business model for the department for the next 10 years. The benefit is that financial planning for the department is directly related to reality.

In other circumstances, it may be more appropriate to restrict the programme to just the highest priority projects needed to achieve the *blueprint*. In our case, however, the total approach seemed to yield a greater degree of control. The progressive approach has paid off in the longer term since each element has been introduced individually and 'cemented in' before proceeding to the next. It proved impossible to do everything in one go.

A bespoke PMIS tailored to the needs of the department proved essential

The information about the programme plan and the business model is held in a bespoke PMIS comprising a comprehensive relational database, report writer and graphics facility. The standard PC project management packages and spreadsheets used at the start of the programme proved inadequate for the job, and are being phased out as the PMIS comes on-line. The aim has been to provide a suite of linked databases so that all programme management information comes from a single, managed source.

Only after the introduction of programme management was the ability to understand both the current and future business achieved. Programme management is now catalysing a radical reappraisal of the 'business' which will lead to extensive business process re-engineering to arrive eventually at the desired future *blueprint*.

With perfect hindsight, we would probably have started programme management a year earlier, and increased the amount of consultancy involved with a view to shortening the implementation time.

3.6 Benefits gained by the business from the programme

The main benefits gained by the department from the introduction of programme management were as follows:

- provision of a single programme-level focus welded the Strategy and the portfolio of projects together

- we were able for the first time to view the overall development situation on a regular basis, to document and address the high level programme issues, to manage risks and take control generally instead of always reacting to events

- the use of tranches concentrated on bringing high payback projects forward into the first tranche of work, thus maximising benefits and increasing the payback to the organisation

- regular reporting of progress, or lack of progress, at Director level, concentrated minds on delivery and on making things both happen – and work!

The tranched programme plan and the monthly progress report have proved really successful in focusing both managers and staff on short term deliverables within the Strategic context. This focus was completely absent before the introduction of programme management into the department. The following are further benefits:

Programme-oriented cost management now in place. Programme cost control is now established as the link between individual project costing and the management of the department's budget. This provides for a clear view of where the money is going thus reducing the risk of (unintentional) cost overruns and ensuring that the scarce funding is now used to best effect to achieve tangible benefits from the programme.

Realisation of benefits is being positively and dynamically managed. Through programme management, the realisation of programme benefits is being positively managed instead of it just being assumed that they will 'happen' by themselves.

Ability to assess the impact of change. The introduction of programme management, supported by the PMIS, provides for a rapid and accurate assessment of the impact of any significant programme change – often a cut in funding imposed on the department by the organisation!

Planning and managing the change to the business. Programme management is leading the planned production of the new business *blueprint* under sponsorship at the highest level.

Providing support to senior management decision making. Programme management provides the department with the definitive management information about the programme. In particular, programme management has been demonstrated to be of great benefit in identifying and containing the unexpected. It supports senior managers in setting priorities and giving direction. It helps with the supervision of multiple projects and ensures that the impact of high level change on business operations is co-ordinated

The transition to new systems is managed. Programme management enables the business to continue to work efficiently while the business benefits from changes are delivered.

3.7 Benefits from using the programme management process	The programme management process is applied department-wide as documented and published in the programme management plan. The main benefits of having a systematically-applied, documented process include the following:

- the department has a single point of focus for programme management

- the documented approach is understood by all. It is bespoke and continually updated in the light of experience

- a clear distinction is made (because the approach to programme management is well defined) between Strategy/programme level and individual project level information

- there is a single source of information about the programme leading to consistent responses to executive level enquiries. In fact, commendation

about the '... timeliness, accuracy and consistency ...'
of the programme information supplied to top
management has recently been received!

3.8   Costs and resources
The CCTA guidance implies that a minimum of three
staff are required to fill the positions on the Programme
Executive with the department's PSO providing the
necessary support. However, this is clearly a 'steady
state' situation. Additional, experienced, resources
proved necessary to facilitate programme start-up.

More specifically, the resources consumed involved an
experienced principal consultant full time as programme
manager for the first 18 months with the individual
undertaking skills transfer to the department's nominee.

A dedicated benefits manager was appointed and he also
supports the organisation's accounts department. At
budget time this post is augmented with short term cost
analyst consultancy support to assist with the 'number-
crunching'.

A dedicated design authority person was appointed who
reports, in line management terms, directly to the head
of Projects branch. Although this is a slightly different
reporting line from that contained in the CCTA
guidance, the responsibilities are similar to those
recommended.

Support consultancy is contracted in to cope with peak
workload at baselining and budgeting time. Typically
this support is provided in 30-day portions, which
averages to the equivalent of one full-time person – but
of course, all different people!

Initial attempts to utilise the Projects branch PSO did not
prove satisfactory, due to a combination of cultural
problems and over-arching demands from project teams.
Accordingly, a dedicated programme control section was
set up initially with two staff, but shortly to be
augmented by a third (PMIS programmer/cost analyst).

The role of Programme Director naturally fell to the
department's director who held Senior Technical roles on
several of the major PRINCE projects as well as holding

line management and budget responsibility for the department as a whole. The Programme Director thus provided a considerable degree of authority and gave programme management the level of authority it deserved.

The following PMIS facilities were procured: Hardware: (4 x 386 PCs, A4 Laser Printer, A3 Laser Printer, Hewlett Packard A0 colour plotter; Software; Programme Management Information System (PMIS) containing bespoke facilities built onto OpenPlan project management software using FoxPro application development tools, plus Microsoft Office standard PC applications.

The budget for the setting up of programme management worked out, as a percentage of the total cost, as being comparable to the cost of setting up project management for a typical individual project. In our case the cost of the 10 year Strategy was in the region of £100m and the £500k charges incurred in the setting up of programme management over the first 1½ years only represented 0.5 per cent of the total 10 year cost. The initial setting up costs involved the provision of consultancy, the development of the PMIS and the provision of PMIS hardware and software. The ongoing cost (using the department's permanent staff to whom skills had been transferred over the first 1½ years) is tentatively estimated to total another £750k over the remaining 8½ years bring the total cost of programme management to 1.25 per cent of the total 10 year cost of the Strategy.

3.9   Where next?

The introduction of programme management has been a considerable success for the department. However, we recognise that it is an on-going management discipline that will continue to develop and become more refined in the light of experience. This parallels the introduction of quality management into any organisation – one never finishes!

For the next twelve months we intend to build on lessons learned. The past twelve months have been about gaining understanding, and the next twelve months will be about gaining and improving control.

3.10   Constraints

The approaches and actions described in this case study reflect an actual situation that is still developing. For this reason, it should be noted that:

- the rate of implementation of programme management was adversely affected by restrictions in both resource and available funding and consequently, as at April 1994, not all CCTA recommendations are yet in place

- the prior organisational situation affected what could be achieved and changed how the implementation was carried out compared to an 'ideal' situation.

3.11   CCTA commentary

This case study highlights that where there is a need to win the 'hearts and minds' of those involved with authorising, controlling and running projects, a progressive approach to setting up programme management can succeed.

The CCTA guidance recommends that IS strategies and business process re-engineering should be business-led, not IS-provider-led. The activity of identifying and selecting programmes is conducted at the strategic level, from which are provided the aims, objectives and policies to ensure that programmes meet business needs.

Since one aim of this programme was to gain control over projects that were already running, the Programme Identification and Programme Definition phase activities were conducted in parallel. CCTA's guidance recommends that the two phases are seen as distinct sets of activities, so that a programme is scoped and its objectives defined before detailed work on the programme definition is undertaken. Programme Identification may reveal that more than one programme is required: the business case for each is critically examined, and separate Programme Briefs written and a Programme Director appointed for each.

The Programme Management Plan that was progressively developed for this programme contained programme level procedures as they became defined: including benefits, risk, issues and quality management, project initiation and closure, and programme level guidelines and procedures. The Programme Plan contained the programme's schedule of projects, with project interdependencies explicitly shown. A *blueprint* (the description of the intended way the business will work in future) was drawn up separately.

In the CCTA guidance, the Programme Definition Statement, which must be kept up to date throughout the life of the programme, contains the programme objectives, the *blueprint*, descriptions of projects required to implement the *blueprint*, execution plans, risks and benefits descriptions and management plans. It documents the financial justification for the programme and how it will be resourced and controlled, and how the transition to new systems and ways of operating the business will occur.

The Programme Manager's role is to ensure the delivery of outputs from projects to time and cost, to monitor progress, to ensure efficient use of resources, and to manage interdependencies between projects and to 'plug the gaps'. In the circumstances described in this case study there was some tailoring of the responsibilities of this role to fit with the existing structures of centralised project control.

This case study discussed the limitations of (PRINCE) Project Support Offices in supporting the programme in the collection of data on programme progress. A PRINCE Project Support Office is a central function that co-ordinates and supports the work of projects, to improve project planning.

A Programme Support Office may be set up to collect, co-ordinate and analyse management information to support the Programme Executive, normally with computerised information gathering. A Programme Support Office can service both the programme and individual projects, where separate Project Support Offices cannot be justified. The Programme Support Office may carry out other supporting tasks, including, holding master copies of programme documentation, analysing dependencies between projects, and establishing consistent reporting and control procedures.

4 Managing change in the working environment

This case study was provided by
Touche Ross Management Consultants

4 Managing change in the working environment

4.1 Introduction

This case study describes how programme management contributed to the restructuring of a large organisation in the public sector. Historically, the organisation had developed into a complex three-way matrix. The programme aimed to simplify the organisation to ensure profit centre managers were directly accountable for their sphere of operation (which would typically be a business with a turnover of £100m), while building a quality organisation with greater focus on the customer. We discuss several of the 'softer' issues involved in the programme management of the forty or more projects comprising this major reorganisation initiative.

The business had, with limited success, made previous attempts to streamline its organisation. At an early stage the board identified key factors in making successful the changes it required as being:

- defining a *blueprint* that gave a simple yet robust structure that focused on single point accountability

- ensuring a quality organisation that gave a better focus on the customer

- delivering these benefits as quickly and effectively as possible, while managing the risks inherent in making such sweeping changes. A particular issue was to ensure that the business kept running smoothly while the changes were taking place

- putting in place an organisation and procedures to manage the change.

The case study focuses on the last of these, and on how this contributed to achieving the other critical success factors.

The board of directors assembled a group of key managers (the Design Team) from the business to form a team that would design in outline the shape of the new organisation and subsequently lead the implementation of it. This was a major undertaking, affecting the working lives of 130,000 staff throughout the organisation. The completely new structure would entail different ways of working and cultural change. To put the new organisation into place required the involvement of well in excess of a hundred project managers throughout the UK and a two tranche approach over a two- year period. Consultants were appointed to advise the Design Team on programme management arrangements, to manage the programme control office, and to design and run a series of 50 management training change workshops for the top 600 managers in the new structure.

4.2 The situation that gave rise to programme management

The programme of change could not be run as a unitary project directed from the centre. Since a prime consideration in the emerging organisation was the establishment of autonomy and accountability for the new profit centres, the changes had to be driven in a manner reflecting this autonomy, ie each new profit centre would run its own change project. A balance needed to be struck between a totally prescribed organisation, without buy-in by the staff, and an uncoordinated 'free for all'. Therefore, a programme management approach was adopted (see Figure 4.1). This approach gave benefits in the key areas of co-ordination, safeguards, momentum and progress monitoring.

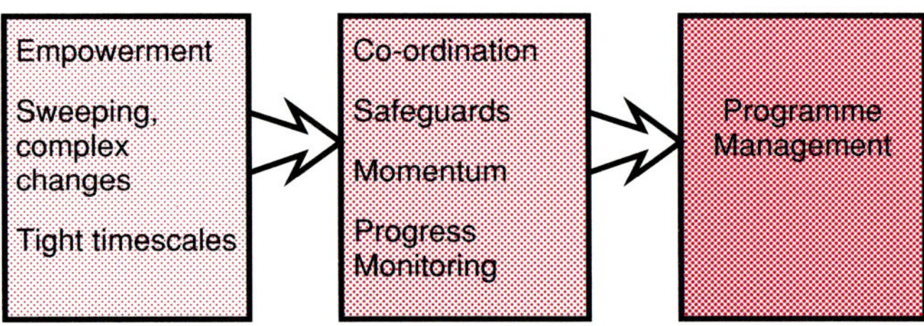

Figure 4.1: The situation that gave rise to programme management

Co-ordination. Clearly there was a need to co-ordinate the work of independent teams each working to develop their new operating arrangements. However, co-ordination was also needed in respect of three further matters:

- reacting to changes imposed from outside the change programme. It was important to respond to external market influences in a measured and consistent way for the whole programme, rather than having separate (and possibly conflicting) responses from individual project teams

- ensuring a common approach to the work by providing planning templates for the project teams. Although each profit centre had its own unique characteristics, there were many elements common to the majority of the profit centres. Providing an overall programme management umbrella across the projects ensured that lessons learnt in one area could be applied effectively and quickly to others

- providing guidance and support to the project teams. The number of project managers involved meant that inevitably many appointees were limited in their experience of this type of work. A key role for consultants working with our programme management team was to support and guide the numerous teams and individuals through, for example, training sessions in the skills and techniques required.

Safeguards were needed for two reasons. The extent of changes that the business was experiencing gave significant risk that some organisational aspects would be overlooked. The programme management team provided a backstop that ensured all these changes were covered. A further safeguard, this time in respect of the programme itself, was to ensure that the many dependencies between project teams were managed.

Momentum had to be built up to deliver results on time and ensure all the project teams kept in step. As well as ensuring that such interdependencies were managed, the programme approach ensured that individual projects were, where appropriate, ring-fenced, which allowed project managers to focus on their own work.

Progress Monitoring was required principally to ensure overall delivery of the programme benefits according to the planned timetable, but also to help ensure progress was maintained in the constituent parts which needed to proceed at the same pace to maintain continuity.

4.3   Programme organisational arrangements

Once the principles and conceptual design for the new organisation had been decided, Managing Directors of the new businesses were appointed, and each established a project director for their business, who each in turn appointed a project manager for the development of each profit centre. This is shown in Figure 4.2.

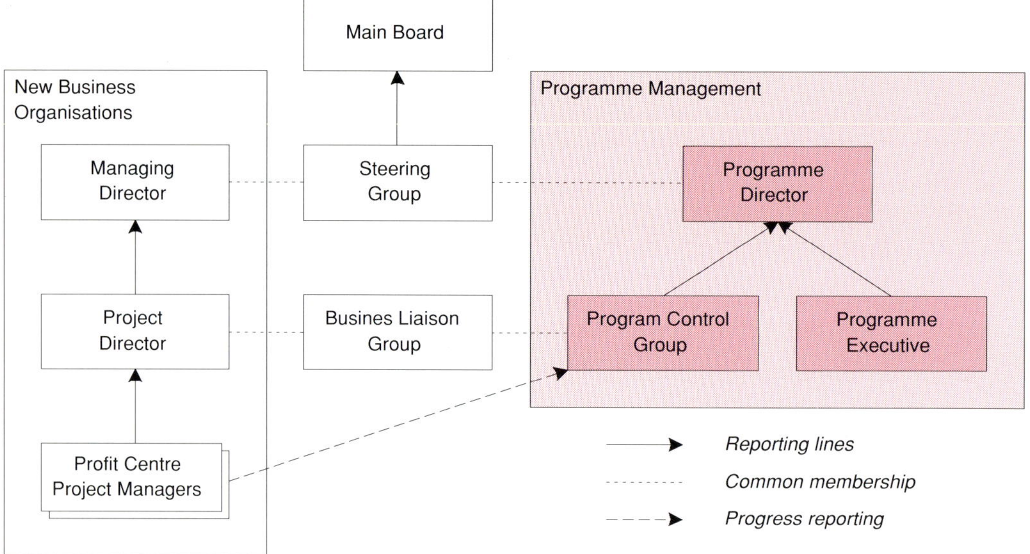

Figure 4.2: Programme organisational arrangements

The Design Team was kept together to undertake the Programme Executive roles, and report through the Programme Director to a Steering Group. This Steering Group consisted of the Chief Executive of the organisation, the board members with responsibilities for the restructuring programme, the Finance Director and the managing directors of the new businesses – again reflecting the need to focus on the direction the organisation was taking.

The Programme Executive consisted of twelve people, drawn from different parts of the business. This meant that the range of knowledge to carry out the programme management roles of Design Authority and Business Change Manager effectively was available in the team.

Having put in place the basic organisational structure for managing the programme, an important element was still missing. The Programme Executive needed to reinforce the communication link with the emerging profit centre teams. There were two aspects to cover.

First, the co-ordination of plans, progress and interdependencies was satisfied by establishing a Programme Control Group (PCG). One of our external consultants was seconded onto the Programme Executive to lead the PCG (as 'Programme Controller'), because most of the in-house project managers were relatively inexperienced with this type of restructuring work.

Second, co-ordination of the many policy decisions needed was satisfied by establishing a Business Liaison Group which consisted of key members of the Programme Executive, the new business's project directors and the Programme Controller. This group resolved issues arising between businesses (such as which existing groups would go into a Central Services Division, and which would be absorbed by the new profit centres, who should own and manage which assets, etc.). They acted as a filter so that only the most important or controversial decisions needed to go to the Steering Group, as well as ensuring that all the key people were kept up to date.

4.4 Project interdependencies

One specific role of the Business Liaison Group was to identify and resolve conflicts on interdependencies. This was a big issue because there were around forty separate projects underway, all interrelated in that they were each trying to piece together a new organisation which depended on taking elements from the old, complex, organisation. Action was taken on a number of fronts to address the problem.

First, the majority of the profit centre plans needed to reflect similar activities, so the PCG developed plan templates, which not only ensured that all key activities were covered, but also ensured some consistency between plans, making subsequent monitoring much more manageable. It was found to be important to get the right balance in the templates – if too sketchy they added little value to the teams, and if too comprehensive, the recipients would not buy-in to the process.

Second, a technique that became known as 'cross-slice planning' was used. Central plans were set up for recognised critical areas in the programme, including for example the consultation process, which was a comprehensive method of determining formally, with the unions, who did what in the new organisation. Other examples included safety validation, accommodation and finance. It was important to set up these central plans so that the individual project plans could be checked and synchronised against the timetables and requirements of these critical areas, and then subsequently monitored against them.

Third, regular formal reporting and feedback cycles were established by PCG to provide a management framework aligned to the monthly Steering Group meetings chaired by the Chief Executive.

However, with the number of interdependencies that existed it was only practical to manage the most critical on a formal basis. Establishing the 'cut-off' for formal monitoring was not easy, and it was quickly recognised that good informal networking between the project teams was vital to managing the numerous detailed local links. Every opportunity was taken by the PCG to strengthen this aspect of the programme. This was a demanding exercise as many of the teams were geographically dispersed, had a tremendous amount of work to do, and were inexperienced in major project work. Effective communication channels – both formal and informal – are always a key factor in making a change programme run smoothly.

This question of informal networking was linked to the wider issue of communications generally. This is recognised as being a significant factor in the success of most programmes. In this case, a particular barrier to good communication was the pressure of work on most participants which led them to neglect cross-team communication. Efforts to address this included:

- ensuring regular information was provided by the centre, and from the main board in particular

- setting up the programme organisation (as described above) to ensure that at least the most critical communication channels were kept open on a formal, and regular, basis

- ensuring that the control system covered the 'checks' and 'prompts' and information flows described in the following sections.

In many ways, it could be argued that the success of the programme was more dependent on ensuring that the critical communication channels existed and were used effectively than on anything else. The control process was relatively simple. What really made it happen was the continual efforts made to coach, support and direct resources throughout the programme structure and the organisation as a whole.

4.5 The 'softer' issues – resources and skills

One of the 'softer' issues that arose on the programme became known as the 'Brick Wall Syndrome'. This concerned keeping the project teams alert to the possibility, and indeed probability, that something unforeseen would occur which might cause a major disruption in the programme, or even jeopardise the programme's success. There were events outside the control of the programme team members (such as adverse press publicity from a small number of staff disaffected by the impact of the changes on them) which could only be managed at the time they occurred. There were other events within the team's control where risk management and contingency allowances were appropriate.

In large change programmes affecting the whole of an organisation, many project managers must be drawn from the organisation to implement the programme. Most organisations do not have the project management skill base in sufficient quantity to manage such a huge change. In this case, over a hundred project managers were required and inevitably many of those appointed only had 'hard' project management experience, if indeed any. Some came from line management positions in personnel and employee relations, because of the importance of these areas. Most, however, had not been through a similar large change process before.

Therefore, a vacuum existed in terms of most project managers' experience and ability to recognise and anticipate pressure points at critical times during the programme. This was something that project management training could only tell people about – it could not provide the experience upon which a project manager's intuition is based. This inexperience, unfortunately, still led to short term thinking and planning, so that even the more obvious problems were sometimes missed.

So what was done to overcome this inexperience? The following response was made:

- an important role for our consultants and PCG was to make sure that project managers were continually thinking ahead and developing the detail of their plans as they proceeded. This was achieved by keeping pressure on them for forward information – by placing an emphasis on rolling planning. This at least avoided the obvious pitfalls, if not the totally unexpected

- a further step involved prompting the project managers to carry out regular risk analyses on their projects – looking for weaknesses within their plans, and ways of managing them. They were asked to be particularly aware of interfaces between the projects forming the whole programme. This, typically, was where problem areas arose – most soft projects are not conducive to tracking interfaces through a conventional dependency route, especially when plans are held locally and geographically apart. The networking and effective communications processes already mentioned were, therefore, reinforced to reduce the risk of missing dependencies

- we were advised to build more contingency into the plans – additional time, and more resource. Since organisational 'one-off' soft projects tend to cover completely new ground each time (particularly from the organisation's perspective), resources are usually more difficult to estimate than for their 'hard' project counterpart, and therefore more likely to be underestimated.

Finally, a small number of the appointed external consultants with relevant experience (headed by the secondee leading the PCG) became intimately involved with the programme, so that they were knowledgeable and committed enough to regularly raise concerns, and help avoid periods in the programme when complacency or over-optimism might set in.

4.6 The 'softer' issues – monitoring and control

Resources and skills are just one aspect of managing 'soft' projects. A further area involved how, during the execution phase, the project should be kept on track – the 'softer' issues surrounding the control and monitoring of a large reorganisation programme.

Projects are traditionally controlled with three well recognised measures – time, cost and quality (or specification). Because, throughout the life of projects, pressures will exist which bring these three factors into conflict, they are often referred to as the triangle of balance; see Figure 4.3.

Judging the right level of balance is also vitally important in making a programme work, from achieving the right level of devolvement and buy-in, to sustaining commitment to the success of the whole programme, its ideals and goals.

A key programme benefit involved the implementation of a quality organisation. Thus, understanding the triangle of balance in terms of individual project objectives was particularly important. For example, if quality required more time to achieve, then the Design Team had already determined that the balance would fall in favour of quality at the expense of time (or programme delay). This message, however, needed careful communication to prevent poor quality from becoming an acceptable excuse for programme delay.

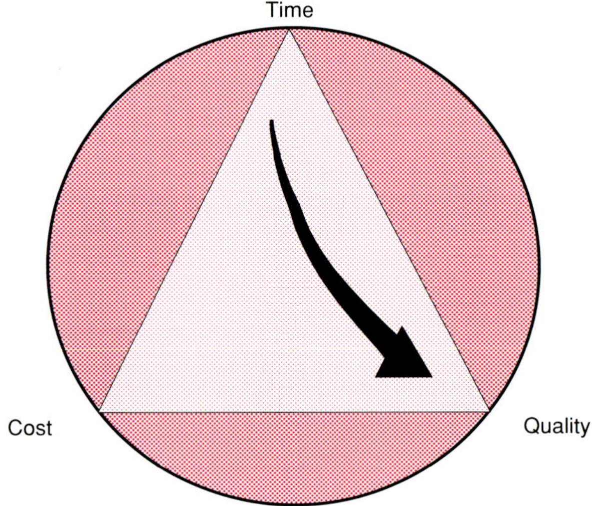

Figure 4.3: The triangle of balance

An interesting example of applying the correct level of prescription was the way in which the project management system for each of the planning teams was adopted. Although a recommendation was made from the centre for a particular package, there was no compulsion that any particular system should be used, and it was left to local managers to decide (since the individual plans were not dynamically linked through the software, the actual package used was not terribly important). Under these circumstances of devolved responsibility all teams opted for the recommended package.

We were advised that on other programmes where a software package has been prescribed much greater resistance had occurred (which in turn had manifested itself in ways often detrimental to the overall programme). We realised that the way in which prescription was to be handled from the centre was a key judgement that needed to be made by the Programme Director at an early stage, since it influenced his ability to monitor progress many months later.

Finally, the reporting of reliable progress information on a regular basis to ensure good programme control was only achievable:

- once robust and consistent plans were in place (and baselined), and the commitment the plans represented was fully owned at the local level

- once arrangements for reporting had been put in place and were fully understood.

Without one of these important control ingredients, a reliable picture of where the programme stood at any time in relation to the plan was difficult to establish. This then left unclear what action was required to control the programme in order to keep it on schedule.

In reality, one could not in these situations be absolutely sure of the reliability of the progress information. If a team wished to fabricate or distort its progress information to the centre, then there was little (in an environment promoting devolvement) to stop it. Essentially, the units were relied on to exercise their recently endowed powers and act responsibly in the way they reported to the centre. Peer pressure was used to encourage reliable reporting of progress – not declaring late running was perceived as letting themselves down, as well as colleagues in other devolved units with whom they were linked.

Of course, techniques were available to 'detect' rogue results from individual units, but use of such techniques was discouraged, and was certainly no substitute for achieving ownership and buy-in to the whole programme.

4.7 Managing environmental change – the lessons learnt

In conclusion, it is clear that programme management has an important contribution to make in managing and controlling any major organisational change initiative. We believe the experience gained, and lessons learnt from this large organisational change programme have wider application elsewhere:

- programme management maintained a relevance to the business objectives and aims of the organisation, and how they might be impacted by external events

- it provided both balance and perspective to the suite of individual projects within the programme, through a common understanding of the wider picture

- it put pressure on individual project managers to deliver to their own Time, Cost and Quality targets, provided a focus for their interdependencies with other projects within the programme, whilst overcoming the tendency for individual projects to lead a life of their own

- finally, programme management enabled project managers to concentrate on their own projects, leaving the programme management team to worry about interactions with the outside world.

Indeed, we believe these lessons apply to any set of projects where the real world is changing.

4.8   CCTA commentary

The key success factors for this programme were identified by top management: there should be a *blueprint* defining what the future business would look like; there should be a focus on the customer and quality; there could be more flexibility in handling future scenarios than with individual projects; benefits must be delivered and risks managed, while the existing business was kept running.

Because of the setting up of the new profit centres – in which the change programme was rolled out separately – the programme management organisation that was put in place needed to liaise with profit centre managers: it was necessary to set up additional liaison groups for communications and programme control. Much of the work of liaison was in tracking progress and interdependencies. The liaison group involved members of the Programme Executive (who had shared the responsibilities of the three Programme Excecutive roles between 12 staff) and representatives from the change implementation projects in the cost centres.

This programme was successful because the effort to ensure lines of communication, both formal and informal, was effective. The case study also shows that enabling rather than coercing individual project teams works to good effect.

5 Scoping the programme

Section		**Page**

This case study was provided by
Ernst & Young

5 Scoping the programme

5.1 Summary

If a programme is to be constructed and managed as a coherent entity, its scope needs to be defined. There is always a great temptation to grow the coverage of programmes until they are unmanageable. Most importantly, the larger the size of a programme, the greater the areas of risk and the less the likelihood of meeting the required objectives in a timely manner.

The scope of a programme is a management concern. Major tenets of CCTA's guidance on IS strategy are that a strategy should be achievable, affordable, manageable, understandable and measurable. Since an IS strategy articulates one or more programmes, the same characteristics apply.

The parameters that are helpful in determining appropriate scope are only in small part technical. Even where the major ingredient of a programme is the introduction of technology, modern technological architectures and infrastructure rarely demand large scale, big-bang implementations.

What really matters is that:

- a programme is identifiable, with clear objectives

- there is clear accountability for success

- the costs, quality, benefits and timescales of the programme are managed

- the relationship with changing business circumstances, needs and priorities is maintained

- the interdependencies between component projects and activities are understood and tracked

- the programme and its progress are managed on the basis of risk management.

Programmes do not appear out of thin air. There is always a trigger – for example, a review or assembly of business objectives, a response to a political initiative, a distillation of market intelligence. Where information systems and technology are involved, programmes are usually constituted as the means of implementing some or all of the portfolio of projects arising from a business/IS strategy.

Many IS/IT strategies in the past have concentrated on the IT projects and technical elements. Management of change issues was frequently overlooked – to be reacted to at a late stage and sometimes with the consequence of programme abandonment. Use of IT strategy methodologies invariably resulted in large complex implementation plans focused on centralised systems. But the key problem was that the 'logical' approach to driving out the scope of applications and projects was primarily based upon data use, not on the basis of accountability for benefits.

A seemingly inevitable consequence of this is that the driving force behind IT implementation has fallen to the IT provider organisation, and the implementation has frequently been seen as an imposition on the recipient businesses.

In this case study, a prime tenet was to align programmes with accountability structures. In the main, this was achieved by aligning with business groups. There were, however, some corporate programmes that could not be aligned in this way. On the other hand, subjecting apparently corporate programmes to scrutiny resulted in most being redefined as business group responsibilities.

This case study concerns the scoping of programmes – not as an academic or technical exercise – but with the aim of ensuring the most effective delivery of benefits from investment. The results delivered from this case study correlate closely with CCTA guidance – essentially a combination of the key elements of the 'Programme Brief' and the 'Programme Definition'. The former was a direct product of the IS strategy exercise. The details of the 'Programme Definition', including the definition of the vision or *blueprint*, were produced through work undertaken by each business unit immediately following the strategy study. Assistance to newly created programme managers was provided by members of the strategy study team. CCTA guidance refers also to a 'Programme Benefits Review Report'. We took great pains to ensure that mechanisms were put in place which encompassed reporting on previous years' (tranches') achievements. The annual process of reviewing the programmes embraced this benefits reporting.

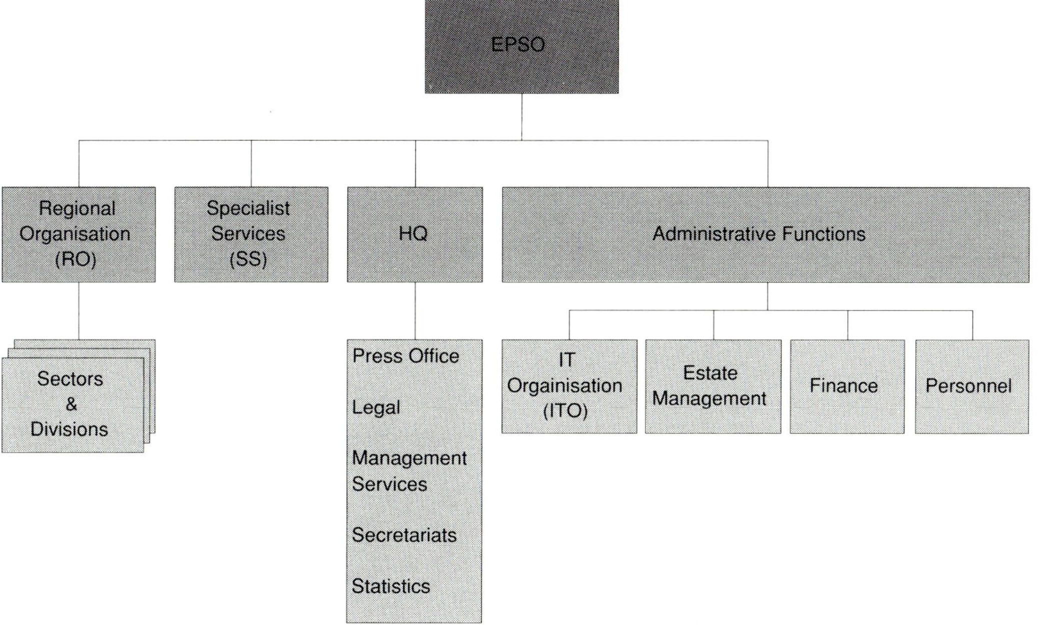

Figure 5.1: Organisation of EPSO

5.2   Background

The starting point was an existing information strategy, some four years old. The need was recognised for a fundamental review of this strategy and a conversion to an Information Systems strategy. The information strategy was owned by the Management Services organisation (MSO), and had become somewhat divorced from IT planning and delivery undertaken by the IT provider organisation (ITO). The strategy review, which built the foundations for programme management, was undertaken by a joint team of consultants as prime contractor, with assistance from a subcontractor and a multidisciplinary team from our own organisation.

Our organisation is a vital part of the public service, referred to here as the EPSO (Essential Public Services Organisation). See the simplified organisation chart in Figure 5.1.

The main operational arm is dispersed geographically with functionally similar units based around local offices. These are organised primarily for line management purposes into local sectors and, within sectors, divisions. This 'customer facing' part of the operational activities (referenced here as the Regional Organisation, RO) is supported by Specialist Services (SS) which for a range of reasons are not dispersed along with the main operational units. It is important to note though that SS is not an administrative function, but part of the core business of the enterprise. The operational part of the business (RO and SS) accounts for the bulk of the manpower.

A range of administrative functions exist in support of the business. The detail of these is not relevant to the case study except that they comprised (at the end of our review):

- the IT Organisation

- Estate Management

- Finance

- Personnel

- HQ (including a variety of functions covering Press Office, secretariats, legal, Management Services, etc).

The existing information strategy had only marginally taken into account the operational aspects of the business. It had, however, identified system requirements of a major scale for:

- Estate Management (ESTATE project)

- Financial Management (FINEST)

- Personnel (PERSIST).

In addition, the IS work programme included a major operationally orientated project. This was concerned with the collection of operational information to be used locally within RO for its mainstream activities and for management information, also to be used and updated within SS (operationally) and to be the basis of statistical collection by HQ. For the purposes of this case study we shall name this ROSS.

Although there was some user involvement in steering and driving IS projects, this was patchy. The dominant role was taken by ITO which in effect dictated the pace and nature of IT development. To its credit, it had developed a technical architecture to embrace the organisation as a whole and was proceeding with a roll-out of the network and associated facilities. An extraordinarily large IT Steering Group (some 20) were involved in prioritisation of projects and associated spend. This was renowned to be ineffective.

A very relevant aspect was that the organisation was beginning a process of major organisational and directional changes. At the time of the case study, the full impact of these changes was yet to be revealed. What was already clear was that 'empowerment' and delegation were to be key principles for adoption and that this would impact right across the organisation including the operational activities.

The process of developing the new strategy is not of itself of relevance to scoping programmes. Only those elements that were relevant are referred to in this case study. However, it is important to note that our intention was from the outset to constitute programmes rather than individual projects and to put in place mechanisms, policies and practice that would enable accountable management to be sustained.

5.3 Identifying with objectives

The relative importance of business objectives can change over time. A major determinant of the priority for investment attached to a programme (or a constituent part) should be the degree to which it supports the achievement of objectives. This implies that the priority of a programme will change over time. A traditional business case which simply compares costs and benefits is an inadequate basis for making investment decisions.

It should also be remembered that the objectives will vary from one part of the business to another. If one considered a power generating company, the main revenue generating business would of course be electricity generation (through power stations), with profits being deployed in the identification and development of new ventures. The objectives attached to the power stations would include reduction in unit costs and would probably be linked with strong corporate control over running costs (including investments such as IT).

On the other hand, the objectives for that part of the business concerned with new ventures would not be focused on unit costs (rather development of new profitable revenue streams) and would be unlikely to set stringent cash and running costs control so high on their objectives list.

Within EPSO, in parallel with the establishment of potential IS needs, we invested much effort in assessing and documenting categories of benefit and in classifying objectives. In the latter case, these were based upon a corporate mission/strategy statement which articulated the main operational objectives of the EPSO. Cash releasing savings (and objectives) were separated out from operationally driven objectives.

At this stage we were not concerned with the relative priority of objectives. This is because in such a large and varied organisation, priorities vary across component business areas. In addition, we took the view that this was a task to be undertaken by business and programme managers (ie those responsible for apportionment of resources according to priorities).

We did, however, make suggestions on the relevance and weighting of specific business objectives to different parts of the organisation. Cost minimisation (and therefore cost reduction) consistent with required service levels ought to be an important objective for any administrative support function. This argument we applied to the ITO, Estates, Finance, Personnel and HQ functions. However, quality and effectiveness of service were the prime drivers in RO and SS.

One of the effects of going through a process of linking potential programmes to objectives is to identify where there is internal conflict within a programme. This can arise if the scope of the programme is cast too wide and especially if it is assumed to satisfy the needs of different organisational units with different drivers and priorities. This is not to say programmes should always be contained within organisational units. Within any level of 'business group' one can usually find that there are another five potential business groups claiming similar status. However, a programme that does not align to a single span of control assumes a level of complexity which is to be avoided if at all possible.

An example occurred with the existing FINEST project (or programme). This was to embrace the introduction of new finance systems to ensure proper control and co-ordination of cash and financial reporting and to provide local managers with means of managing their own budgets. The aims of the two main groups (central finance and local managers) are widely divergent. The former tended towards a large central and centrally managed system (covering all possible complexities) with data extracted from local units. The latter was (or wished to be) focused on simple local systems that would enable local managers to collate and manipulate their own data and to provide aggregated information to central finance.

This divergence would have inevitably led to dissatisfaction by one or the other party. Given that the project was being driven by Central Finance, it is evident which one was likely to suffer. Attempting to combine divergent needs has another effect which was already evident with FINEST. Provision costs rocket; Rolls Royce solutions are constructed to meet user needs for a Mini.

Getting the scope of a programme right involves looking within and looking at the objectives being served. If there is divergence (as in this case study example), consideration should be given to splitting it and assigning separate ownership. The overall programme (for example, introducing new financial management systems and procedures) may continue to be required to ensure co-ordination, in which case separate projects addressing separate needs could be constituted. Alternatively, completely separate programmes could be initiated.

During the review, we identified the issue of conflicting objectives and as a result, the scope of FINEST was constrained to the central finance role. A new project was launched to address the local management needs. Because the final shape of delegation within the EPSO was at that time not clear, an interim 'tool kit' approach was adopted for local budget management.

Clear accountability for success

Perhaps this is the most important principle for programmes. A nominated role/individual must be accountable for achievement of the programme's objectives. The EPSO was embarking on both structural and cultural change. The main underpinning of this was the introduction of greater accountability aligned to delegated authority.

Ultimately the new regime of empowerment would mean that the management of a business group would be faced with making decisions about allocation of available resources comprising all resources necessary to discharge its remit. Constraining-type policies would be minimised. Although budgets would continue to be split between revenue and capital, management would be able to choose between different forms of capital spend in accordance with its local priorities and circumstances. Theirs would be the decision on whether to spend on equipment or vehicles or computers, and theirs the decision over use of manpower, overtime and other running costs.

Although the full impact of these changes in management was probably some years off, the view was taken that the IS portfolios arising from the IS strategy should be aligned to and subsequently programme managed by business groups. These groups should be the same as those adopted for management accountability. As such, IS/IT was paving the way for the new responsibilities and freedoms that would operate in the future.

Reinforcement of this view was provided by our survey of business managers and users, which had revealed that they felt distanced from IS decision making which had been handled almost exclusively by the ITO. In addition, the ITO had managed the funds for IT (capital and running costs). The fact that not all projects undertaken by the ITO had been successful was not in itself unusual, but the lack of involvement by some customer businesses was, and was probably a major contributory factor. The view of many business groups was that systems were developed which were far too complicated because attempts had been made to satisfy every requirement, even whims. Critical examination of requirements against the costs of their satisfaction was not apparent. In order to place responsibility with the customer business groups, migration towards a charging regime within which customers held the greater part of the budget, was regarded by us as inevitable and necessary.

It was clear that this was going to be a painful process for customer business groups and ITO alike. It would also take a number of years if the migration was to be managed sensibly. However, the first step was to identify the scope of the business groups and then as far as possible to align the IS programmes with them.

Accountability is, of course, much more than responsibility for priorities and resource allocation. Perhaps the key factor is accountability for delivery of benefits (which is referred to below). This links with having clear objectives for the programme which will in turn reflect the specific needs of the business group and its management. Achievement of success demands clear-sightedness and the authority to make decisions covering a wide range of resources and activities, for example user training, pace of roll-out, management support, process changes, job changes, which stretch far beyond the remit of an IT provider. It also demands weighing of options carrying different expenditures and different benefits. Technology cannot be assumed to be the best solution.

5.4   The problem of corporate programmes

In our case study, we hit the thorny issue of 'corporate programmes'. Much of the development of IS portfolios had been straightforward once we had established the management and structural building blocks of EPSO. New requirements could be aligned fairly simply to the business group structure and the associated objectives. However, there was a range of existing programmes and projects which emanated from the original strategy or had emerged and been 'scoped' under the old structure. The coherence of these was based on functional similarity or information commonality. The problem was that there was no single identifiable sponsor and no-one specifically accountable for their success. Artificial allocation of ownership can give rise to the problems of FINEST referred to above, where one perspective on requirements may dominate.

The additional problem with corporate programmes is that of allocation of resources. Should the organisation top-slice business groups' budgets to ensure adequate provision? Should the funding of the corporate pot take precedence over business group demands? Should business groups be permitted to withdraw financial support for corporate programmes?

We decided to take a robust view of corporate programmes, ie that in the ideal world there would not be any. We started with a list of some six or seven so-called corporate programmes. These included:

- FINEST

- ROSS

- the infrastructure project PSION

- Research and Development and Standards activities in ITO.

In each case, we scrutinised the objectives they were intended to serve, and most importantly, the beneficiaries, ie those parts of EPSO that would gain through successful delivery. A mapping of programmes to accountable business units is shown in Figure 5.2.

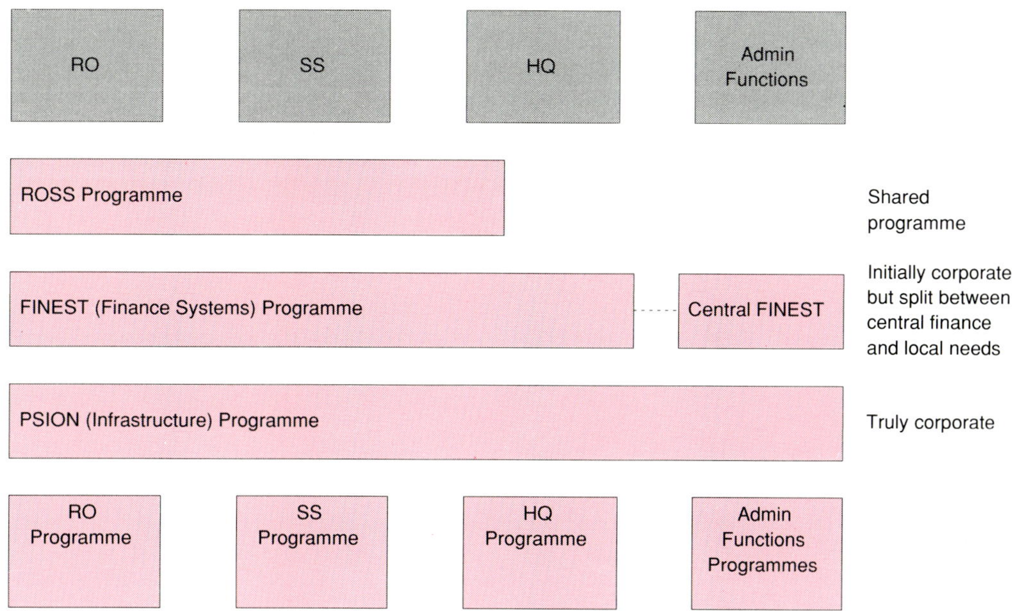

Figure 5.2: Mapping programmes to accountable business units

In the FINEST case, as referred to above, the analysis suggested a realignment of the core programme to Central Finance's requirement whilst enabling, separately, provision for local needs.

ROSS presented particular difficulties. It had developed a life of its own, had consumed a large amount of available IT resources and was beset by problems. In effect, ROSS was ownerless in any meaningful sense. Although individuals had taken responsibility for steering it, they were not accountable in the sense that the health of their part of the business depended on it.

The beneficiaries of successful implementation covered RO, SS and HQ but to differing degrees and it could be argued that the image of EPSO as a whole would be directly affected by success or failure. Each part of EPSO had a different perspective on what it was supposed to achieve and what the priority of those business objectives were. We could identify that the objectives for ROSS were shared between RO and SS and it was these two business groups which were the prime beneficiaries.

The HQ interest (primarily statistics, statutory requirements and comparative performance) had created a significant degree of additional complexity and to some extent had dominated thinking. Assessment of the objectives and beneficiaries suggested to us that there were actually two coherent programmes – one concerned with the operational needs and associated change, and the other with central information needs.

Clearly, ROSS was not truly corporate, because not all business groups stood to benefit. It was however, a shared programme and therefore could be treated in a manner similar to the approach we adopted for corporate programmes.

If one addressed the ROSS related needs of each business group (assuming a fresh start could be made), the system would be significantly simpler and the costs of implementation an order of magnitude less: a building block approach could have been adopted, enabling a simplified architecture of the system and its interaction with business groups.

We were not able to resolve completely the issue of ROSS within the context of the strategy. However, through programme management principles we were able to put in place the foundation for change. For ROSS as with all corporate programmes which survived the scrutiny, we calculated the full costs associated with it and then apportioned these to the business groups which would benefit. The tabulation in Figure 5.3 illustrates the allocation of corporate programme costs to business groups. Simple methods of apportionment were used based upon the size (manpower) of each business group and a valuation of benefit.

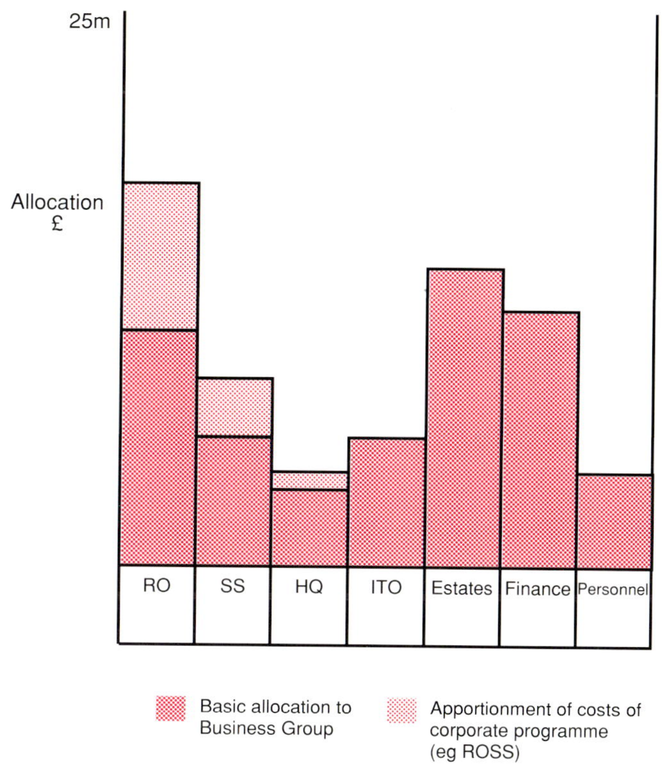

Figure 5.3: Openness of allocations (showing corporate programme apportionment)

Each business group could then see the costs of its share of the programme and relate these to the costs of its 'new' portfolio and our estimated costs of providing ROSS functionality by alternative means. The Business Groups were then able to consider the case for continuation or substitution as a share holder, accountable for both the consumption of resources (set against competing demands) and the delivery of benefits. Clearly a key factor in this decision making process was to be the degree of confidence and inherent risks attached to the existing or alternative programme.

Another observation about ROSS is worth making. Within EPSO it was regarded as a project (an IT project) and was managed by the ITO. In actuality it represented a significant programme of change orientated to changing the way in which part of the operational activities of EPSO – its key business processes – would be undertaken. Whilst the specific IT solution under development might have been recognised as inappropriate and a different approach adopted, the business change programme would (in this case) continue.

Programmes are about managing risk and taking on board decisions on options throughout the programme life. The lack of **accountable** programme management driven by the beneficiary business groups was probably the main cause of problems arising with ROSS.

The results of the scrutiny of corporate programmes was that only PSION and R&D survived. All others were refocused to align with business groups, entailing, in some cases, fragmentation of previously created programmes and projects.

5.5 Costs benefits and timescales

The management of costs, benefits and timescales are essential elements of programmes. The scope of a programme may be materially affected by these considerations. A programme must be affordable. Given known or likely availability of resources overall, the enterprise needs to be able to allocate sufficient resources to enable successful pursuit of the nominated programme. Clearly these resources are not just financial. The task of scoping the programme should take account of the manpower required and the specific skills and people involved.

Furthermore, there will be competition for those resources from competing programmes, including the delivery of current services. ROSS was an example where ultimately the scope of the programme was influenced by cost considerations. The original programme (pre-review) had incurred substantial costs. We had established that if the objectives of the programme could be modified slightly, the costs of satisfying them through a fresh approach could be dramatically reduced.

Benefits realisation is perhaps the most important element of programme management. Identification of achievable benefits, and the tolerances that might be attached to them in scale and timing, help determine both the scope of the programme and the pace of change that is implied. In EPSO, the demand for new systems was significantly tempered once the customer business group was forced to be specific about the business objectives being supported and the actual benefits that would accrue. Part of the approach in introducing programme management was to make business managers account for benefits realised in the previous year as part of their case for resources in subsequent years. This shifted the emphasis from business case preparation (as an end in itself) towards measured benefits realisation. Confidence that benefits were achievable became the cornerstone of critical examination of the scope (and priority) of programmes.

The business groups (programme managers designate) volunteered a marked descoping in the functionality expected once they realised the impact on costs and timescales for delivery. We were able to show that quick wins based on the provision of core functionality would enable change to be managed in a more controlled way. Resource constraints could be coped with and additional benefits could be realised at a later stage.

Where major changes to business operations are ultimately envisaged, adoption of a tranched approach can be extremely helpful in winning hearts and minds, not only with those directly impacted by the change, but also with those with authority over the provision of resources.

5.6 Changing business circumstances

The EPSO was embarking on a radical process of reform and restructuring (a programme in its own right). Clearly, it would be foolish to embark on or continue with an IS programme that ran counter to or was to be made redundant by predictable changes. We demonstrated that existing programmes had not been kept in line with changes to the business and its priorities. There was a danger that the new programmes that we had identified and constituted could also suffer from the same problem. The annual review process (including scrutiny and reprioritisation of programmes and their component parts) which was instituted, we believed, would reduce this danger.

However, keeping track of changes in the business environment and being able to revise the direction and content of programmes requires a 'highly responsive and intelligent' programme management role. The fundamental support for this was documentation of the underlying business assumptions for the programme and the impact should they subsequently change.

5.7 Interdependencies between projects and activities

In scoping a programme, one needs to define all the component projects and activities. Not all of these are projects with hard products (a feature which distinguishes programmes from project based approaches). The strategy review within EPSO was in effect a programme whose objectives were to establish better and more focused planning and management of IS investment. Although we could define the hard products of strategy (the portfolios, the policies, the plans, etc), we recognised that change would only be achieved through winning hearts and minds. Accordingly, we assigned the task of 'communications' – a soft activity – to a member of the team who helped to identify allies and opponents and to construct a campaign of consultation, workshops, feedback sessions, articles, etc. The important lesson learned was that traditional product based planning would have been difficult to apply to soft activities given the absence of prior knowledge about distinct products. Where continuous stream activities are elements of the programme, it is important to allocate the resources required and to build review points into the programme plan to ensure that objectives are on track.

A programme will normally contain a high number of options and decision points. Interdependencies are often related to these decision/review points, perhaps rather more than to prior completion of products/activities. Follow-on projects and activities will be dependent on the results of **decisions**. In consequence, a plot of the constituent parts of a programme tends to be divergent rather than convergent. In scoping the programme, care needs to be taken to allow for changes to scope and content as progress is monitored. However, a clear *blue print* – a description of the required result (as opposed to product) and the objectives to be attained – is the basis for monitoring and adjustment throughout the programme.

During the EPSO strategy review, as well as identifying the portfolio which constituted each business groups' programme, we also articulated the 'vision' for EPSO as a whole and assisted the business groups in defining the vision for their programmes. This vision statement is included in the business groups' annual statement of programme objectives and achievements.

5.8	**Risk management**	One of the programmes within EPSO was referred to earlier as ROSS. This provides an example of where risk analysis and management techniques provide an important input to programme scoping. Assessing the risks to achievement of a programme's objectives (for example: staff resistance, technical uncertainty, scale of change) may well result in the realisation that there is an unacceptable level of risk. Descoping or extension of timescale or provision of additional resources or activities may well be ways of reducing risk to an acceptable level. In the case of ROSS, which was a programme well into the final stages of completion, a detailed assessment of the business risks attached to the programme resulted in a fundamental shift in its content, coverage, and technology base. Clearly, for programmes at the stage of initial scoping, risk assessment will not be at a detailed level, but is still helpful in protecting against overstretch and 'grand plans'. At the time of programme review, it is a powerful means of putting programmes and their overall objectives back on course.
5.9	**CCTA commentary**	It is suggested in this case study that the scope of a programme is geared to the delivery of achievable benefits. Not only must benefits be achievable, but the organisation must identify individuals who will be accountable for their delivery – and a senior manager committed to getting the whole programme to deliver.

Scoping may show that there should be a logical division of strategic requirements into a number of implementable programmes. Tranching enables and reinforces the emphasis on delivery of benefits, the release of funds, the attention to core functionality and suitable review points for realignment of the programme's scope for changes in the business environment.

Early risk assessment will help to keep a programme's scope within bounds. Also, changes to the business environment must be reacted to – the programme cannot simply plough on without regard to such changes.

Attention to core functionality and accountability is eased if programmes are aligned to business units (which may need to be set up as part of the programme). Existing strategies and programmes may need to be re-examined in order to achieve such accountability and achievability.

Some programmes (or projects within programmes) are corporate, affecting more than one business group, but this case study recommends the approach that business units should have a stake in corporate programmes, even to the extent of a client/provider relationship: the stakeholding business group must release or withhold the resources and skills for the corporate programme to continue its execution, and will only do so if the corporate programme is delivering its benefits.

To help a programme win hearts and minds, resources will need to be allocated to soft issues such as marketing and identifying impediments to the programme.

6 Using a *blueprint*

This case study was provided by
CSC Computer Sciences Ltd

6   Using a *blueprint*

Programme management is the management of large-scale complex change within an organisation. Such a scale of change usually impacts right across the organisation, and the process of getting there is further complicated by the fact that the final result is often unpredictable at the outset. The broad range of organisational interests that need to be involved in such a scale of activity, allied to individuals' different backgrounds and orientation, result in many and varied interpretations of the transition path. These different requirements need to be aligned.

It is the initial objective of programme management to ensure the necessary alignment and thus to establish a sound base for the transition. It is our contention that a *blueprint* has a major part to play in this. Further, we would venture that the lack of such a *blueprint* to promote a consistent view of the target state of the business is one of the major causes of programmes veering off course and even failing.

In programme management the *blueprint* sets out how the business will operate when the programme has been completed. The *blueprint* must be refined and maintained throughout the life of the programme. The *blueprint* expresses the future in the form of models to represent the various components of business operation, typically: processes, organisation, facilities, data, applications, technology, and their interrelationships. These can be supplemented by measures of operational performance defined to ensure that the desired benefits are realised by the programme.

This case study aims to illustrate how the use of a *blueprint* during a strategic programme initiative can address the issues raised above, and more, by:

- providing a high-level focal point for where the programme is heading

- providing a basis for prompt option evaluation when a change of direction becomes essential for the programme to deliver optimum benefit

- providing a basis for determining the degree and impact of change for each option evaluated.

6.1   The situation

We recently undertook a major change programme to adjust our market focus and make more effective use of our resources. The programme made use of a *blueprint* in a variety of ways, not only to focus programme activity but also to educate and communicate.

We are a financial service company providing a range of investment style products to individual investors. We have a nationwide branch network of approximately 100 offices, each of which serves as a direct sales point, as a base for sales agents, and as an administrative centre for sales and servicing support operations. The company employs 10,000 people in total.

Tougher market conditions and, to a lesser extent, legislative changes recently caused us to reorganise into four business units, acting mostly independent of one another. This change was successful in fostering a more entrepreneurial spirit, as a result of which we have retained market share. The latest strategic review, however, indicated that with our existing costs the current way of doing business would not be sustainable. As a result, a new programme was established to improve the company's methods of operation with two specific directives :

- refocus all of the business divisions to local markets based on geographic areas

- implement corporate support functions where there was commonality.

Having recently completed the divisional structuring programme, not all of the four business division heads were in accord with the scale and nature of changes being proposed. An early goal of the programme was therefore to convince the principals that there were benefits across the board in seeking further operating improvements.

6.2   The role of the 'visionary' *blueprint*

Given the nature of the changes sought, there was no prescriptive model or precedent from which to work. Each participant had their own perception of what would be required; it was an important aspect of programme management to ensure that these views were consistent enough for all to play their proper part. The central role of the *blueprint* was in providing a landmark for this consistency by creating a vision to work towards.

As the programme developed the *blueprint*'s role changed to meet the need at the time. We shall consider these variations in the context of the phases of programme management activity. The phases and the variations in *blueprint* role are illustrated in Figure 6.1.

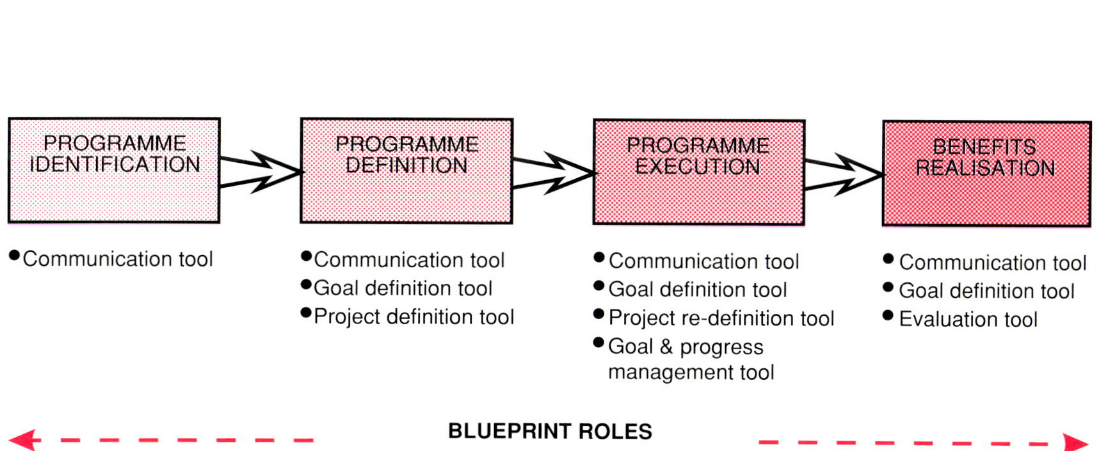

Figure 6.1: Varying roles of the *blueprint*

Programme Identification – during this phase the aim was to decide the scope of the programme and obtain a consensus of agreement to this scope. To do this the consultants advised us to create a vision of the future business operation in the form of a *blueprint*, which outlined a concept model of the future state of the business. The *blueprint* at this stage was used as a learning tool, helping the programme principals to set sights on what could possibly be achieved, to introduce alternative visions for the business and altering perspectives on the business (for instance from viewing the business as a set of activities to viewing the business as a set of processes). When the 'art of the possible' was perceived, the way was open for selecting the best option and defining it in detail during the next phase of programme definition.

Programme Definition – during this phase programme management objectives were to establish the baseline for the programme; to establish the infrastructure for management; to document the programme scope; and to define the delivery mechanisms. The *blueprint* helped with these by representing the change 'footprint', in other words by providing a view of the nature and scale of change to be introduced. High-level models were used to educate all the main programme participants and change agents, and to act as the vision for how the business would operate in the future. Once agreement had been reached on this vision between the Chief Executive, the divisional MDs, senior divisional management and their direct reports, and the core programme management team, it was an easier task to assess the full scale of the programme. This aided the determination of optimum tranches in which to deliver business releases, and provided an initial view on the key risks. A secondary role for the *blueprint* during this stage was in identifying natural owners for projects – an unanticipated bonus.

Programme Execution – throughout the delivery and integration activities that make up the Programme Execution phase, programme management objectives were to ensure that the business changes were delivered. The *blueprint* assisted in two ways – first in representing a current view of the future business, which served as a yardstick for monitoring achievement, and second as a tool for impact analysis, providing a broad view on the implications of any major change to the programme. In practical terms the *blueprint* was reviewed on a quarterly basis to ensure its currency with changing programme goals. This exercise was also useful in critical path analysis. The plans at both project and programme level contained elements of 'planned contingency', but the *blueprint* enabled alternative approaches to be modelled when risk mitigation necessitated modifications to the vision of future business. Once control factors indicated a change was required, plans could then be adapted to the modified vision. By cross-referring the two elements, plans and the *blueprint*, a better picture of the status of the programme was constantly achieved.

Benefits Realisation – following each tranche of delivery, programme management objectives during the Benefits Realisation phase are to assess achievement and refine plans for future tranches of the programme. For this the *blueprint* provides the basis for measuring achievement against goals and as a continual control on the direction of the programme towards realising its objectives.

6.3   The *blueprint* approach

The general approach taken was that the *blueprint* should be an integral programme management tool and as such required both active management by the programme, and participation by key representatives of the business to ensure its validity. The approach worked well for this type of programme as the various components – planning, scope control, benefits modelling, *blueprinting*, quality control, and risk management – could be inter-related, their relative significance varying according to the programme phase and, of course, status at any time.

This case study shows how the *blueprint* was used as a 'visionary' tool to educate participants in the new ways of thinking, to communicate programme goals, and to assist as a control mechanism for assessing the impact of change and monitoring progress.

Figure 6.2 gives an overview of the blueprint approach. In this section we shall examine the objectives, and application of the *blueprint* will again be examined from the chronological viewpoint of the programme phases. Note, however, that the Programme Execution and Benefits Realisation phases were combined in this particular example. The nature of the programme was such that pilot running led to staged roll-out as the new business areas were developed. Programme tranches were designed such that pilot and roll-out included elements of benefit evaluation on a continual basis. The range of activities associated with the phases of

Programme Execution and Benefits Realisation were treated as a sequence of development, integration, assessment and realignment steps within Programme Execution.

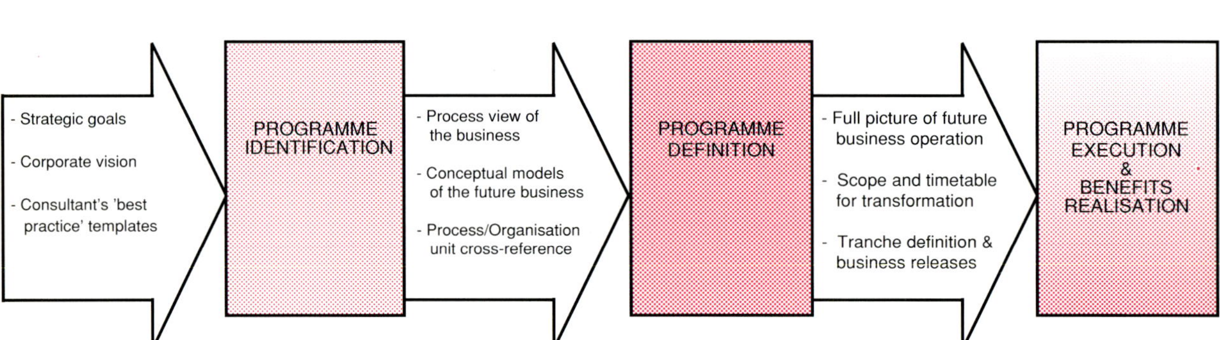

Figure 6.2: Approach overview

Programme Identification

A 'visionary' *blueprint* was used primarily as a learning vehicle with the objectives of:

- proving that the medium to long term business objectives could not be met with current ways of doing business

- introducing a 'process' perspective on the business, and in so doing helping to illustrate the dependence of one function on another in satisfying business aims.

As a starting point the goals from the strategic agenda, which had been drawn up during a strategic review of operations, were applied to the consultants' 'best practice' templates to develop an outline 'visionary' *blueprint* for the programme. The strategic agenda goals provided a suitable focus for future business models that were radically different from the current business operations, by providing improvement targets and reinforcing the impression that different ways of doing business were essential. Examples of the goals set were, in summary :

- 40 per cent reduction in unit cost of sale

- market share increase of 10 per cent in total business within three years

- reduction in number of branch offices by 10 and consolidation of all business units into local markets based on eight geographic regions.

Process overviews of the current business operations, a process-to-organisation 'map', and conceptual flow models of certain aspects of the future business were used to formulate the *blueprint*. Responsibility for the production of the models was shared between a modelling tool specialist, business analysts and the key change agents. The latter group comprised members of the core programme management team and 'progressive' representatives of the business areas who had skills essential for delivering the successful transformation of the business operations.

A process perspective was introduced through modelling the current state of business operations, and a process-to-organisation mapping which highlighted some of the areas of duplication and potential bottlenecks that could be removed.

In using this approach to prepare the Programme Brief, the *blueprint* succeeded in setting the scene for the Definition phase by breaking down the barriers of thinking in terms of existing organisation functions and obtaining general acceptance that major new ways of working could be introduced via the programme.

Programme Definition

The 'visionary' *blueprint* was used during this phase as a definition vehicle with the objectives of :

- defining the future state to a sufficient level to gain widespread acceptance of achievability

- identifying projects and tranches for programme delivery.

The *blueprint* is a major deliverable of this phase

providing the detail necessary to establish the scope and objectives for the programme. The proposals identified in the Programme Brief were developed into a definition of the future business operations in a form suitable for the plan of action to be prepared.

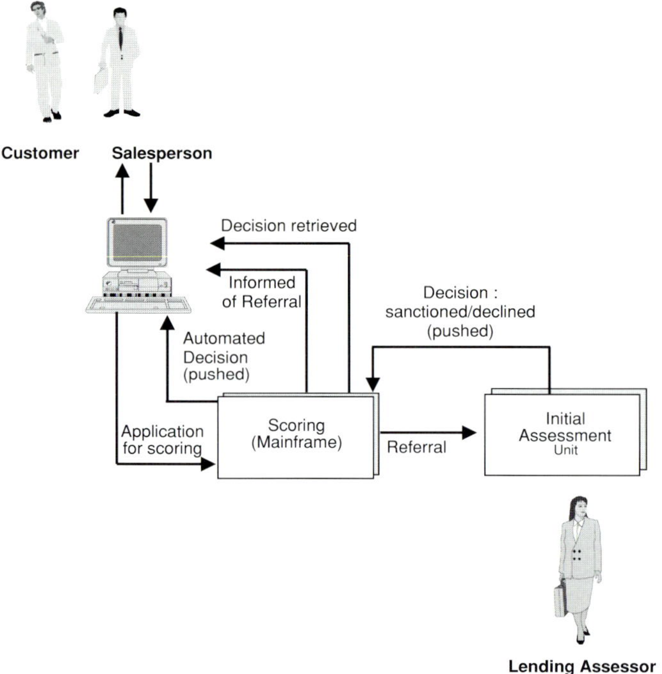

Figure 6.3: Concept model

The outline models prepared earlier were enhanced and built on in order to provide a full picture of the future business operations. These were supported by models of the new organisational responsibilities and of the systems architecture, the latter providing an initial view of the technology and application components to support the future environment.

As an example of the style of deliverable, a sample of the concept models is shown in Figure 6.3.

In terms of practice, the core team mentioned above developed the model views. Workshops and functional work groups then provided the forum for communicating and gaining consensus, during which time the *blueprint* was instrumental in providing focus as the basis for evaluation. The old and new states were then compared as a start point in defining the work breakdown for the transformation itself as well as setting the operational measures that the changes could achieve. Two techniques were employed to represent the transformation and the capabilities necessary to achieve it, illustrated by the examples in Figures 6.4 and 6.5.

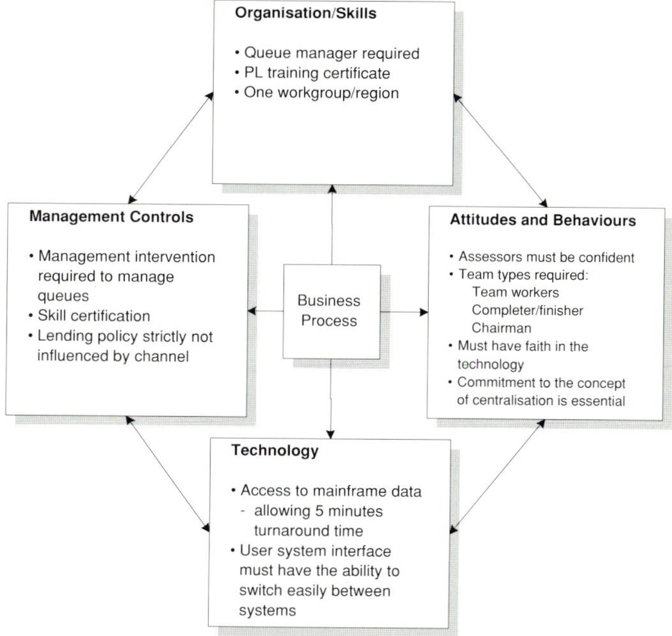

Figure 6.4: Diamond model

The hexagon is used to represent the degree of change across the enterprise as a whole, or, as in this case, within a particular business area. This example profiled the impact of the new way of handling business cases. The model illustrated that process changes would constitute a major part of the transformation effort and that new systems would almost certainly be required to implement the degree of data and application renovation to be introduced. Organisationally, the changes would not be too wide reaching although on further analysis some re-skilling would be necessary.

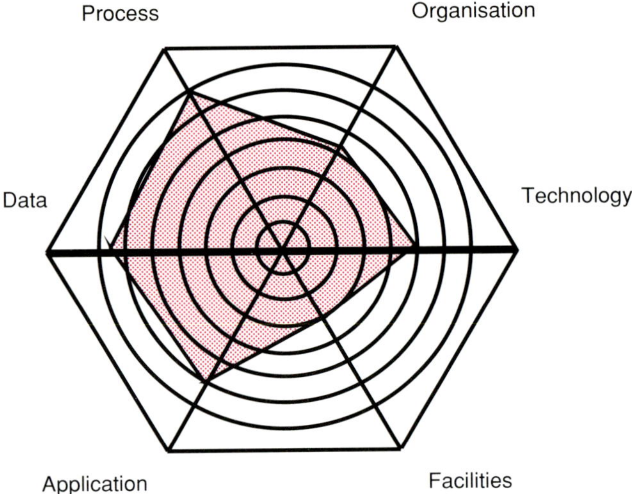

Figure 6.5: Hexagon model

The defined future state and the initial breakdown of the transformation helped the programme management team to determine what the tranches of business release were to be and provided input to initiate the planning process. Involving the key personnel in defining the future business operation helped the programme management team to clearly identify the natural owners of the future business processes. This enabled project management responsibility to be assigned for a number of the programme's projects and responsibility given for the implementation of, and transition to, the new processes.

Programme
Execution and
Benefits Realisation

As the programme progressed through the delivery and integration cycles, the *blueprint* was used:

- to provide an overview for impact analysis of changes to the programme

- to act as a yardstick for delivery measurement.

One of the fundamental uses of the *blueprint* was to maintain a reliable vision of future business operations.

Each significant amendment to the programme was evaluated against the *blueprint* to check whether it affected the end result. It is also worth noting that by maintaining a form of audit trail business benefit evaluation was made easier as benefits were dropped or affected by each change.

Throughout these phases, parts of the *blueprint*, particularly the process and concept models, were in constant demand as educational material when releases were rolled out or new processes piloted. As with its use during the Identification and Definition phases the *blueprint* provided a clear view of the business operation and therefore proved to be invaluable in aligning or orienting participants' perception of the changed business.

During the course of this programme the company acquired another, smaller company with products similar to those marketed by one of the four business divisions. Although its operation was relatively easily absorbed, expanding both product portfolio and client base, the programme had to take the implications on board. One particular aspect warrants mention here as it changed the approach to the process defined for customer service. The acquired company had recently installed a new service based on systems using a combination of display screen and telephone operation; these were used in a highly imaginative style to provide scripted dialogue and full client history from document images. There was initial resistance to the idea of further redesigning the processes to use this approach, for reasons such as:

- *the situation has been evaluated and existing goals confirmed*

- *the new option may work for a smaller company but would inevitably turn out too expensive for the new organisation of the size envisaged.*

Nevertheless the programme management team, in assessing the impact of the change, initiated a study into alternative approaches. An alternative *blueprint* was prepared for the different customer service model and the two options evaluated by a task group which included two representatives from the new company. (See Figure 6.6.) The new process and systems won the day by discussion based on alternative *blueprints*; the task group could quickly evaluate the relative benefits to the point where the decision made itself and had the support of all concerned. (Cost was in fact not an issue as the systems from the acquired company could be adapted more quickly for the client's corporate use than the development plans for the earlier solution.) The *blueprint* was modified to reflect the new future state and the programme plans were adjusted accordingly.

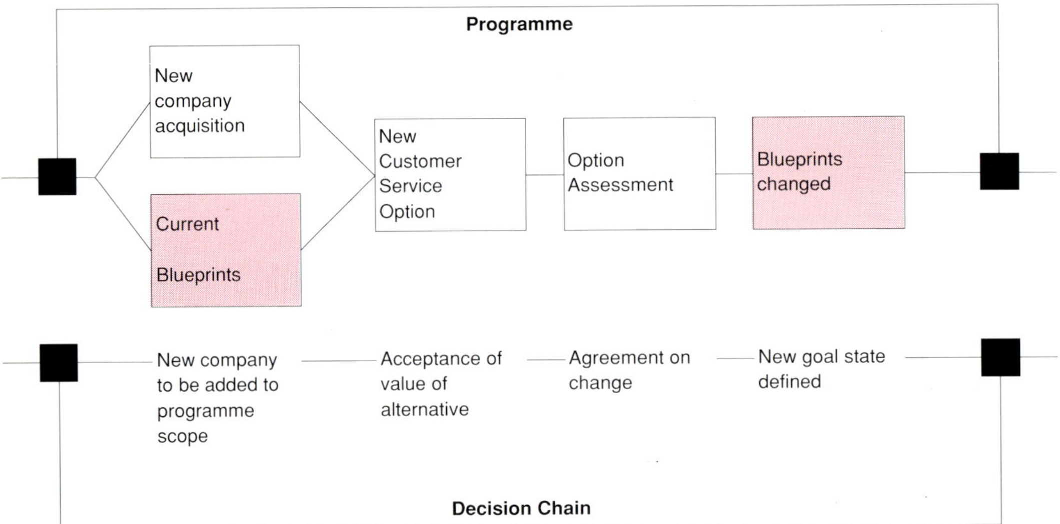

Figure 6.6: Decision on change to the programme

This event illustrates two significant points :

- a *blueprint* can supply a ready means to facilitate impact analysis of any scale of change

- programme management can use a *blueprint* to keep a constant check on benefits to be delivered (it is important that if benefits are no longer going to be realised, or can be significantly improved, a major adjustment to the programme objectives and definition must be considered).

In summary, during the various cycles of delivery and integration that make up the Programme Execution and Benefits Realisation phases, the visionary *blueprint* assisted programme management by:

- providing an overview of achievement against the defined future state

- providing an audit trail of the changes made on the transition path

- providing an initial basis for impact analysis.

6.4 The audiences for the *blueprint* around the programme

Although the *blueprint* provided a focal point for common appreciation of the programme goals, its use and benefits not only varied according to the phases of the programme but also according to the responsibilities of the different members of the programme organisation. Figure 6.7 sets out our view on how different roles within programme management use a *blueprint*.

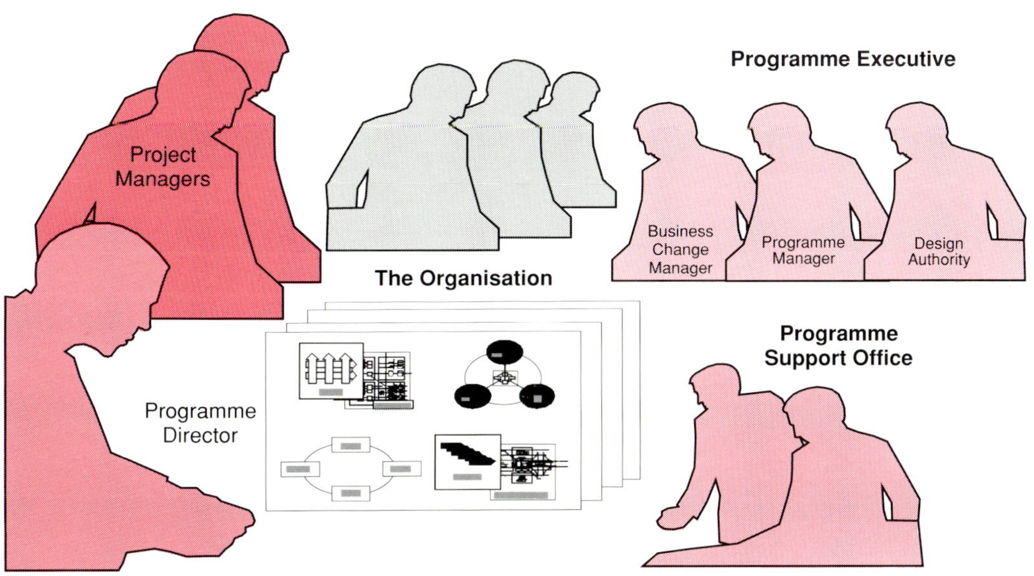

Figure 6.7: Perspectives

To the Programme Director – the *blueprint* can be used in stakeholder analysis (a technique used to identify the major influences on the whole or part of the organisation, their likely perceptions of that area of the business and their potential interactions with it) by raising awareness of the impact of changes in the proposed business area. The sponsoring director uses the models to determine which stakeholders will be affected and to what degree. The findings then provide input to decisions on resourcing and new appointments that would be necessary under the new order.

To the Programme Executive & Programme Support Office – the *blueprint* is a key tool in practically every activity. It provides valuable insight in understanding the overall scale of change; it provides input to the cost-benefit analysis; input to the business case; input to driving out the initial plans; input to project and tranche breakdown. The consensual process reveals natural owners for projects and business processes; and the *blueprint* also provides the basis for impact assessment.

To the Business Change Manager – the *blueprint* is the yardstick for benefits realisation. As a means of monitoring progress it is used to provide an indication of achievement against the defined future state and, together with the programme's model of desired benefits, provides the basis for benefit evaluation. In the early programme stages the *blueprint* plays a part in communications and alignment of programme goals.

To the Project Managers – the *blueprint* is the definer of scope used to draw up Project Briefs. It can be used not only to understand delivery components but also assist in defining project content, interfaces and handover points. It may also be useful in change management at project level depending on the detail of the models employed.

To the organisation at large – the *blueprint* is a common reference point for understanding and 'internalising' what the future may hold.

6.5 Key lessons

General

As a general statement, a *blueprint* adds value – it is not an overhead to the programme.

Some key lessons were learnt from this programme.

Tailor the *blueprint* to objectives, not the reverse.

The objectives of *blueprint*ing, and therefore the nature of the *blueprint*, vary over the life of a programme:

- by providing options for business change and communicating these to the organisation

- as a baseline and control point for progress monitoring and impact assessment of changes in objectives.

Actively involve those people who will be prominent during the transition in the development of the *blueprint*.

The benefits

As a general statement, a *blueprint* adds value – it is not an overhead to the programme.

A *blueprint* helps to define the profile of the key agents necessary to implement change and ensure the success of the transformed operation.

A *blueprint* provides a communication tool and acts as a sound base for aligning participants' thinking and obtaining consensus on programme objectives.

A *blueprint* provides a ready means of quickly evaluating alternative ideas, approaches and forced changes.

The consensual process allied to the use of a *blueprint* is a useful mechanism for identifying rightful owners for transition components (projects and sub-projects) and end results (business processes or restructured organisation components).

The warnings

A *blueprint* can become a means in itself – if the team jealously guards content and does not freely broadcast to programme principals.

A *blueprint* can inhibit a programme's responsiveness to change in aims by going too deep and constraining subsequent re-evaluation of objectives and programme definition.

A *blueprint* can be used to develop an incorrect business bias if the team is not well balanced and widely representative.

In conclusion

A *blueprint* provides the focus for complex programmes of change.

In an uncertain environment a *blueprint* represents a target for all the effort to be properly directed. Additionally, a *blueprint* contributes to the management activities associated with the transition by providing input to the planning process and by contributing to risk and change management.

6.6   CCTA commentary

This case study presents a slightly different perception of how the *blueprint* is developed from that given in the CCTA guidance:

> *The* blueprint *is part of the Programme Definition Statement and describes the business models, operational performance measures, organisation, information systems and support service requirements of the new business operations.*

It should not be thought of as static, but a description that is to be refined as requirements become clearer, and changed if the programme's scope changes during its implementation.

For the programme covered by this study, the early work on programme identification was needed to persuade business managers of the potential benefits of the programme and bring about their commitment to achieving the 'vision'. The *blueprint* was used in scoping the programme: for defining options to select the vision of the future business and for communicating the vision and persuading business managers to sign up to it.

As the scope was clarified, detail was added to the *blueprint* and the programme scope and objectives were defined (which is Programme Definition phase activity).

There was some iteration of this vision identification, and more detailed description as the programme's pilot implementations were rolled out and evaluated.

The *blueprint* was a key document in coping with change to the programme's objective and was used to:

- assess the impact of that change

- generate options for implementing the new business requirements

- overcome resistance to change.

7 The role of the Programme Director

Section **Page**

This case study was provided by
IBM UK Ltd

7 The role of the Programme Director

7.1 Introduction

This case study features a national authority responsible for the provision of a safety critical control service. The service has grown steadily since inception with increases projected for the future. In order to handle the increasing volumes of business a complete rationalisation and modernisation of the service was required, hence the current programme. The case study is written from the perspective of the Programme Director at a point 5 years into the programme with many years still to run.

In tackling the primary factor of demand for growth a number of issues had to be recognised and addressed; they included the following:

- current systems had grown piecemeal over many years

- existing buildings were too small to provide for the new service base – this led to the need to relocate 800 staff

- existing personnel had to be retained – any new location would need to be with their agreement

- the current service was provided on a 24 hour 365 days per annum basis – any transition had to be totally non-disruptive

- the change was too large and complex to be tackled as a single project

- new disciplines and skills would be required to manage a change of this magnitude

- no programme of this magnitude had been undertaken by the authority before, and the authority did not have the personnel to tackle such a programme without outside assistance

- the programme would impact all sections of the authority.

The following sections concentrate on the nature and requirements of the role of the person in overall charge of the programme – the Programme Director. Understanding the nature of this role and the pressures on the individual performing it, is fundamental to an appreciation of what makes programmes succeed or fail.

The programme objectives, approach, organisation and phases are described. Some insight into risks and the perspective of both contractor and commissioning authority is shown, together with a summary of the lessons learned to-date.

7.2 Programme objectives

An early task for the Programme Director is the establishment of a set of business objectives defining what needs to be achieved. In this case the following objectives were set:

- to increase service capacity to handle demands out to the year 2011

- to enhance the level of safety through better levels of reliability, availability, and maintainability of the total system

- to create a low-risk solution with extendible systems architecture

- to be operational by end 1996 with a non-disruptive transition from the old system to the new.

Additionally, because of the programme's major impact on the authority, it was decided to focus as much on the operating costs of the new systems as upon the acquisition costs. This provided a view of the total life cycle costs which was considered important, and gave an opportunity to understand the long-term impact of the new systems upon the operational workforce.

7.3 Programme approach

Following feasibility studies, which were undertaken during 1988 and 1989, the approach to completing the programme became clear. It was understood that the programme would involve a major, complex endeavour, with multiple projects, which only a programme management approach could control.

It was also clear that the programme needed to be reduced to manageable portions. These fell out naturally into the following major projects:

1 Acquisition of a new site with planning consent

2 Construction of a new special-purpose building

3 Development of new high-tech specialised control systems

4 Integration of the new system into the existing UK infrastructure

5 Validation of new operating procedures and provision of training to all staff.

Of these, the most complex project, and the one most likely to be the longest and most difficult to set up and manage, was the development of a new specialised control system. Provision of the following capabilities would achieve the capacity growth being sought:

- increased level of computer assistance

- improved communications capabilities

- re-sectorisation of the domain for which this organisation was responsible, and re-structuring of traffic routes within that domain

- new operating procedures

- improved training and simulation capabilities.

In addition there are a significant number of minor projects all of which need to be closely interlocked in order to ensure a complete service capability when the system becomes operational.

Even with the programme apportioned into manageable projects, the change could not be accomplished in one stage. The programme had to be segmented into tranches of work (see section 7.5: *Programme phases*).

**7.4   Programme
        organisation**

In the past, the practice had been for packages of solutions to be purchased and integrated into operational systems in-house. There were so many elements in this case that it would have taken 500 to 600 of the existing staff if this approached had been adopted. The use of existing staff would have had major ramifications on the day-to-day operations, and therefore was unacceptable. With the decision to apportion the programme into discrete projects it was possible to invite companies to bid for the business on a project-by-project basis. However, some projects had to be retained as in-house projects since the expertise only existed within the authority.

In order to manage the series of projects successfully it was clear that the authority's experience of large systems integration project management needed to be strengthened. New terms such as Life Cycle Costings and System Safety Case Creation, were introduced. The skills to tackle these new disciplines had to be sought outside the authority.

Thus a programme controlling organisation was established at the beginning of 1990 and a team built up from a combination of in-house personnel and personnel from a number of external organisations. It started with the establishment of an initial team of eighty people growing to the current size of one hundred and fifty. This included a Programme Support Office providing administrative support to the programme and liaison between each of the projects and Project Support Offices.

The final but essential component of the management team was the members of the end-user community who were included in order to represent their interests and sign off requirements.

This provided the correct mix of skills and experience to manage and co-ordinate all the programme activity. The team was able to develop the master schedules and the requirements specifications, and to undertake the procurement tasks.

7.5   Programme phases

Programme Schedule

Having set the objective of an in-service date by end 1996 the key project on the programme's critical path was the development and systems integration of the electronic control systems. The involvement of contractors was vital to the successful planning of this work.

The task of requirements capture and definition, which clearly had to be led by the authority's staff, began in 1990 following the feasibility study, and continued through to late 1992. Clearly, if the involvement of contractors was to have been delayed until this activity was completed then this would have left an impossible window for the procurement of the control systems. A procurement strategy was developed which allowed for the involvement of contractors early in the programme whilst still preserving the competitive requirements of a traditional procurement process.

Before the requirements definition had been completed a *Brief to Industry* was sent out to a wide range of prospective suppliers, in December 1990. The objective of this brief was to determine at an early stage which Systems Integrators were interested in bidding for the control systems supply as prime contractor. The brief, together with the feasibility study report, formed the programme *blueprint*.

At this stage the authority also sought to establish the credentials of the Systems Integrators in undertaking a prime contractor role for a £100m+ contract. Minimising the risk to the programme in the selection of prime contractor was an early role for the authority's Programme Director.

This early view of capability, whilst not excluding any Systems Integrator from bidding for the next phase, provided the opportunity for preventing suppliers from investing in a marketing situation for which they were not suited, and the authority's wasting selection time and energy.

Figure 7.1 sets out the programme timescale for the acquisition and support of the new high-tech control systems. After the first tranche of system development a brief 'island of stability' is planned, following which development of the next tranche of the system will take place. There will be several iterations of Phases 3 and 4 (Programme Execution and Benefits Realisation, run in parallel) for each suite of projects. The full programme comprises 150 projects.

Period	Tranche of work	Phase
1988 –1990	Feasibility Study	Identify Programme
Dec 1990 – Jan 1991	Application Brief to Industry	
May 1991 – Jul 1991	Invitation to Tender for Definition of Projects	Define Programme
Nov 1991 – Jul 1992	Projects Definition	
Nov 1992 – Nov 1995	System Development – I	Execute Programme Realise Benefits
Nov 1995 – Nov 1996	System Transition – Go Live	
Nov 1995 – Nov 1998	System Development – II and Initial Maintenance Period	
Nov 1998 – Dec 2011	Main Maintenance Period	

Figure 7.1: Programme tranches and phases

The contractor's perspective

The procurement of the safety critical control systems was a major project within the overall programme. A prime contractor was required to undertake responsibility for the total systems integration of a large number of applications and hardware components which would be sourced from a substantial number of subcontractors.

In this case study, therefore, two roles have been identified – that of the contractor's Programme Director and that of the authority's Programme Director.

Figure 7.2 sets out the phases for this complex procurement together with typical tasks and focus for the systems integration prime contractor in each phase.

Each phase of procurement/supply has clear but different sets of objectives. To ensure continuity of understanding and accountability for decisions within the Systems Integrator, the first person appointed in response to the opportunity should be the contractor's Programme Director.

Phase and Tasks	Focus
Phase 1 IDENTIFY PROGRAMME Opportunity identification and evaluation; requirements; capability; competition; risk; resource; win strategy	BID/NO BID
Phase 2 DEFINE PROGRAMME Proposal development and evaluation; sub-contracting, demos, pricing, negotiations	WIN/LOSE
Phase 3 EXECUTE PROGRAMME Design; development; testing; production; installation; training	CUSTOMER SATISFACTION AND PROFIT
Phase 4 REALISE BENEFITS Operations; maintenance; support	CUSTOMER SATISFACTION AND PROFIT

Figure 7.2: The contractor's tasks for each programme phase

The first task of the contractor's Programme Director is to evaluate the use of investment funding with regard to the opportunity. Such an evaluation must take into account questions such as:

- Are the programme requirements understood in sufficient detail?

- Does the capability exist to undertake not only this bid but delivery of the whole programme of work?

- Is skilled resource available to bid and propose?

- What is the position with respect to likely competitors?

- Is there a winning strategy?

- What risk does bidding pose to the organisation?

The contractor must evaluate these questions objectively and must prepare a reasoned business case with which to persuade his own organisation to provide the funds to invest in the marketing phases. For the contractor the output of this first phase is the decision whether to bid or not.

The second phase is usually one of the shortest, certainly the most intense, and determines whether the contractor's organisation will continue to play a part in the programme or will be forced to a relatively early withdrawal. The phase is characterised by subcontractor selection, pricing, proposals, demonstrations and negotiations. From the customer or end-user perspective, it also sets the baseline for a successful (or otherwise) outcome to the implementation phase. This phase determines how well a common understanding of the systems requirements has been achieved. Shortcuts here will inevitably lead to problems later.

There is no escape from the axiom that ultimately one gets what one pays for. Both Programme Directors (customer and contractor) need to ensure that this message and the consequences of its contravention are understood by their respective organisations.

In the last two phases the main concerns of the contractor Programme Director lie in performance and risk management. The objectives of these are to ensure customer satisfaction and to meet the contractor's corporate goals. Issues in this area tend to lie in understanding where and how things can go wrong, and how to put them right in a timely fashion.

**7.6   Engaging the
Systems Integrator**

With an overall programme duration of twenty-two years, during which period continued support is required of the Systems Integrator's organisation, the selection is more of a 'partner' rather than a supplier. The final result must be a 'win/win' situation for both organisations. The authority's purpose is to get value for money – the contractor's is to make a profit.

For the authority's Programme Director a number of questions need to be asked which relate to the contractor's ability:

- Does the contractor have sufficient financial strength to manage a programme of this magnitude and give assurance of a long term presence?

- Will the contractor carry the financial risk of delays and ultimately penalties and sanctions?

- What is the contractor's business strategy and does it support the needs of the programme?

- Does the contractor have the skilled resource to cover his own programme of work and, in the event that the programme falls behind schedule or subcontractors fail, have enough resource to recover from any problems?

The programme will have a significant impact on the Systems Integrator's own organisation. The decision to establish a long term support structure has implications which go well beyond a normal five-year corporate planning horizon.

The common vision

In a major programme, no requirements specifications can be so accurately defined as to ensure that the system developed will exactly match expectations. In order to minimise cost overruns and ensure no loss of direction the approach was to engage the Systems Integrator as a team player in spirit.

A full understanding of requirements is usually developed during the Programme Definition phase. Engaging the Systems Integrator as a 'team player' needed the Systems Integrator's involvement in the programme definition, but, in order to ensure a competitive procurement for the implementation, two parallel, competitive programme definition studies were run with two potential suppliers.

This added greatly to the workload of the programme controlling team and Programme Support Office but was essential to provide the competitive environment necessary to ensure a reasonable price for the implementation and through-life support.

The Systems Integrator eventually chosen for the execution phase was able to assist with refining the requirements into a realisable procurement specification. This ensured that a common vision of the system requirements was developed which would lead to fewer problems during implementation. Changes during implementation, usually arising out of mis-understandings, are expensive and can bring about both cost and schedule overruns.

The client/contractor partnership

It is as well to understand in a 'partnership' required to endure for twenty-two years that a good working relationship needs to be established between supplier and customer at all levels, from Programme Director through to the team members. This was a key factor in supplier evaluation during the Programme Identification and Definition phases.

Early involvement of potential systems integrators allowed for these working relationships to be developed. Key Systems Integrator personnel were identified during the programme identification and secured for the Execution phase via a key personnel contract clause.

7.7   The basis for pricing

In a typical systems integration programme, the customer is responsible for capturing user requirements and producing a requirements specification. The supplier analyses the requirements specification to produce a systems specification.

This may reflect a system which provides less function than the requirements specification, since there may be requirements that cannot be met with current technology, or for which the cost would significantly outweigh the benefits.

In this case study the systems specification became the basis for the supplier pricing. The systems specification was functionally based, such that exact numbers or models of hardware and software components were excluded. The detail of these would not become available until the programme reached the detail design stage in the Execution phase.

The supplier's designers had the task of finding the least expensive solution to meet the requirements. This led them to select products or services other than from their own organisation, on grounds of cost or lack of a relevant, developed product.

A major part of the price was made up of the cost of the development process itself, including any necessary specialised manufacturing. For the authority to be able to interpret the Systems Integrator's price, some cost engineering skill within the authority's buying team was essential.

Finally, the choice of financial contract needed to be decided. To control cost in this case a fixed price turnkey contract was negotiated. The secret to managing costs under this arrangement is to have a very tight control on programme changes during contract execution.

For the Programme Director, financial risk is a fact of life. It is met in all phases and the Programme Director must have the necessary organisation, personal skills and judgement to address it.

7.8 **Managing the programme**	Essential to the success of the programme is the quality of project management which has been established, both for in-house projects and for contracted projects.

Essential to the success of the programme is the quality of project management which has been established, both for in-house projects and for contracted projects.

Predictability of content and standardisation of process can be assured by the selection of the most applicable methodology. For instance, given that development of the high-tech control systems is a 'real time' software development project it was a mandatory requirement for the System Integrator to apply the appropriate defence standards to control and manage this project.

Similarly, quality can be assured by enforcing the requirement for standards and processes. Conformance to quality standard BS5750 is an overriding requirement of all participants in the programme, with many lower-level specific standards being applied.

However, ultimate success will depend upon the human aspects of project management. Programme Management is a tool to enable communications between all parties on the progress of the projects. It is intended to provide visibility to all aspects of the work. Without the right mental approach from team members, customers and suppliers, the intentions of programme and project management techniques can be easily foiled.

Openness, trust, and communication between people are the keys to success, since much of what has to be done relies on goodwill and encouraging people to meet tight timescales. To do this requires winning the hearts and minds of all. It is the Programme Director's role to set the tone for both the in-house and contractor teams. The relationship between Programme Director and Contractor Programme Director provides the vehicle for enabling these principles. For example, the whole procurement team were encouraged to foster this approach at all levels, with the result that communications were enhanced and a better insight was gained into the progress of the contractor's design and development work.

7.9 Risk management

After the early programme phases and during implementation, the Programme Director must take control of the critical area of risk management. Some key messages can be drawn out.

- Management of risk applies right from the start. Risk identification needs to be undertaken and a control mechanism established

- In order to encourage the identification of risk, openness is essential not only throughout the customer's team but also throughout the contractor's team. It is as well to remember that the responsibility for managing risk is not passed to a contractor simply because a turnkey contract exists.

For the purposes of identifying, analysing and managing risk, a high level of visibility was built into the contractor's activities. Through a full review schedule, which looks at the development progress at all stages, a means was established to understand what was happening within the programme. Care must be taken to ensure that this is not seen as a substitute for the contractor's management responsibilities.

Additionally, while it is sometimes difficult to motivate people to provide measurements of key processes, programme metrics are essential to providing the indicators of the health of the programme and the success of any 'get well' actions.

It should be obvious, though it is not always practised, that any analysis of risk should be wholly objective, in order to identify the root cause of problems and deal with them. Time is always the enemy, and containment actions need to be put in place quickly and effectively. Only with fully delegated authority is this possible (see section 7.10: *Lessons learnt*).

Programme risk areas

A number of risk areas have been identified which are regularly monitored and reviewed.

For example, there are dependencies on other programmes for the supply of software, both from the authority and from the contractor. While delays are not anticipated, the development programme for this software is not under the contractor's control and thus constitutes a risk. Contingency plans have been developed should any delay occur.

Not all requirements will have been fully detailed by the start of the Execution phase. A closure plan has been put in place to ensure that all open requirements are tracked to detailed conclusion.

Risk is further increased in a programme that has many subcontractors but it can be ameliorated by having a prime contractor. This provides the customer with a single point of responsibility. It was the preferred option for this programme, rather than having to deal with a consortium.

Two million lines of code will be developed, and will be combined with many existing commercial packages. Thus the twin tasks of software development and systems integration become the key aspects of the development work. Each requires special attention. Following the initial sizing done at the time the contract was placed, a resizing activity was undertaken and completed, resource levels adjusted to take account of variance, and a full set of progress measurements established.

There are risks associated with system performance. Close control is needed, and the system has been modelled as an early aid to predicting performance. Software will be delivered to the systems integration team in four major builds. As each is delivered, early measurements of the real system will be taken to feed back into the model for calibration purposes. This should ensure that an understanding of the system performance is developed early enough to take corrective action if necessary.

7.10 Lessons learnt

For the Programme Director there are some key messages:

- **delegated authority**: the Programme Director must be given the authority to make the decisions which affect the programme. Only with this authority can decisions be made in line with the schedule of the programme. The clock is always running on a programme and decisions cannot be delayed

- **recruit people with the right skills and knowledge**. Since most large-scale programmes will inevitably involve a particular industry then a good understanding is required of how that industry operates

- **involve end-users**: end-users should be involved as members of the development team in order to prevent unnecessary programme changes

- **involve suppliers early**: early involvement of suppliers is beneficial. Suppliers should be integrated into the wider team to catch the 'common vision'

- recognise that **risk** is not laid off by placing a Fixed Price Turnkey Contract. The risk remains with the Programme Director

- **establish and communicate a clear strategy** and set of objectives to all team players

- **understand your supplier's motivation**: the supplier's objectives may not be in line with those of the programme. A supplier's major motivation is profit

- **management of risk**: the risk to the programme of projects' not delivering products to time, cost and quality is always present. The project management reporting systems must allow for visibility by the programme into risks at project level. Recognition and anticipation of risks are vital at all levels for the effective management of risk

- **allow adequate contingency**. For major, one-off programmes there may be little or no previous experience to draw upon. One should treat estimates of duration, resource, cost and performance with a healthy scepticism, allowing adequate contingency at the project level. The programme needs to recognise the combined effects of project tolerances

- apply continued focus on the **long-term issues**. Given the duration and ultimate impact of programmes of major change, the focus must be more towards long-term issues. For example, requirements should not be allowed to drift, and the original objective must be maintained.

7.11 Summary	The Programme Director's role is challenging and requires a special set of abilities and skills. It should be a senior management appointment, demanding proper empowerment in order to allow fast and effective resolution of issues and, therefore, proper delivery of the programme.

The Programme Director is the single point of responsibility and accountability for success, and thus the quality of the person appointed must derive from a strategic business understanding. Equally, it is against this basis that the performance of the Programme Director should ultimately be measured. |
| **7.12   CCTA commentary** | The Programme Director takes personal responsibility for the programme's achievement, so should be senior enough in the organisation to have the authority to drive the programme through to successfully meeting its objectives. This case study shows the Programme Director role in action: managing the client/contractor relationships and taking the lead in the management of risks, control of costs and attainment of quality.

The Programme Director needs the support of a Programme Executive in these responsibilities: the Business Change Manager will be responsible for driving out the benefits from the programme, and may assume overall responsibility for transition and risk; the Design Authority will ensure satisfactory quality assurance; the Programme Manager will ensure the coherence of the programme, and monitor the projects' effective use of resources (and that outputs are delivered that meet business objectives). The Programme Manager will also assist in the resolution of issues about the programme's definition, the control of costs through the timely management of resource allocation across the programme, and the management of exceptional situations. |

8 Changes in the Programme

This case study was provided by
Andersen Consulting

8   Changes in the programme

This is a case study on how, used effectively, programme management can ensure a successful response to significant changes in requirements during a large-scale Information Technology (IT) programme.

8.1	**Change is the only constant**	The rate of change in the public sector is accelerating, driven by initiatives such as Next Steps, the Citizen's Charter and Market Testing/Compulsory Competitive Tendering. The traditionally predictable environment in which public servants operated no longer exists. The rate of change in society as a whole is also accelerating. This case study examines the impact of change at a macro-level (due to a worsening economic situation during the implementation of the systems programme and a significant increase in the transaction volumes) and at a micro-level (advances in Information Technology during the delivery of the application to end users).
8.2	**The situation**	During the mid-1980s our Agency – whose core business of customer service is supported by IT – began to experience increasing problems meeting our customers' service expectations. The costs of supporting our main operational IT system were escalating, the system was becoming obsolete, and the skills to support it rarer. The Agency decided to replace its main business system.
8.3	**Programme definition**	The programme consisted of a series of interrelated projects associated with the overall goal of replacing the Agency's core business system. The programme contained a series of projects:

- the development of the application software

- the design and implementation of the technical infrastructure

- the design and implementation of a new organisation and new job structures

- the delivery of training to the system's users and support personnel

- the testing of the system

- the piloting and subsequent roll-out of the system.

As such, the early stages of the programme focused on the production of the design for the system and areas of our organisation impacted by the new system. The principal part of the programme dealt with the development of the system itself. The latter part of the programme's execution focused on the implementation of the system in the Agency's offices throughout the country.

8.4   Why was programme management necessary?

The replacement of the system was a very large undertaking. The system controls over 60 million transactions within a year and directly affects the lives of over five per cent of the UK population. The magnitude of the system itself is significant; some 30,000 users access 20,000 terminals in 1,200 locations. The total cost of the programme exceeded £800 million.

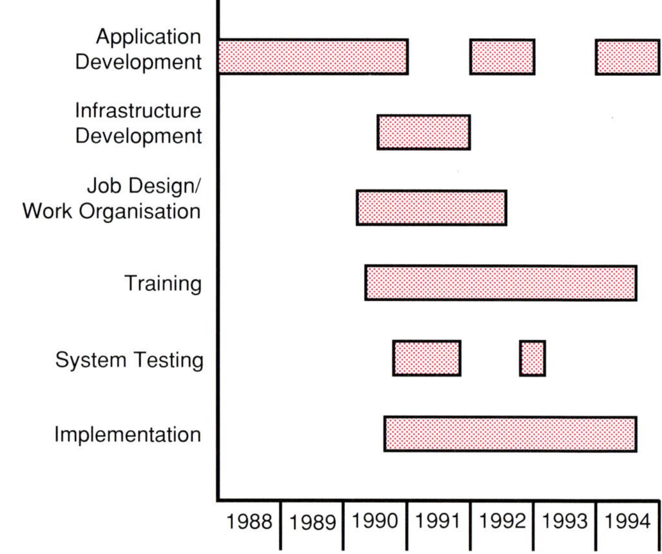

Figure 8.1: The programme timescales

At the outset of the seven year programme (illustrated in Figure 8.1) it was known that effective programme management would be a critical factor in determining its success.

We identified the following reasons for using a programme management approach:

- maintenance of the programme's schedule

- control of the programme's expenditure

- management and tracking of interdependent tasks/projects

- effective inclusion of all critical tasks within the programme's schedule

- ensuring achievement of the business benefits on which the programme was based

- successful introduction of new working practices and efficiencies

- long lead times for the procurement and installation of networks and hardware.

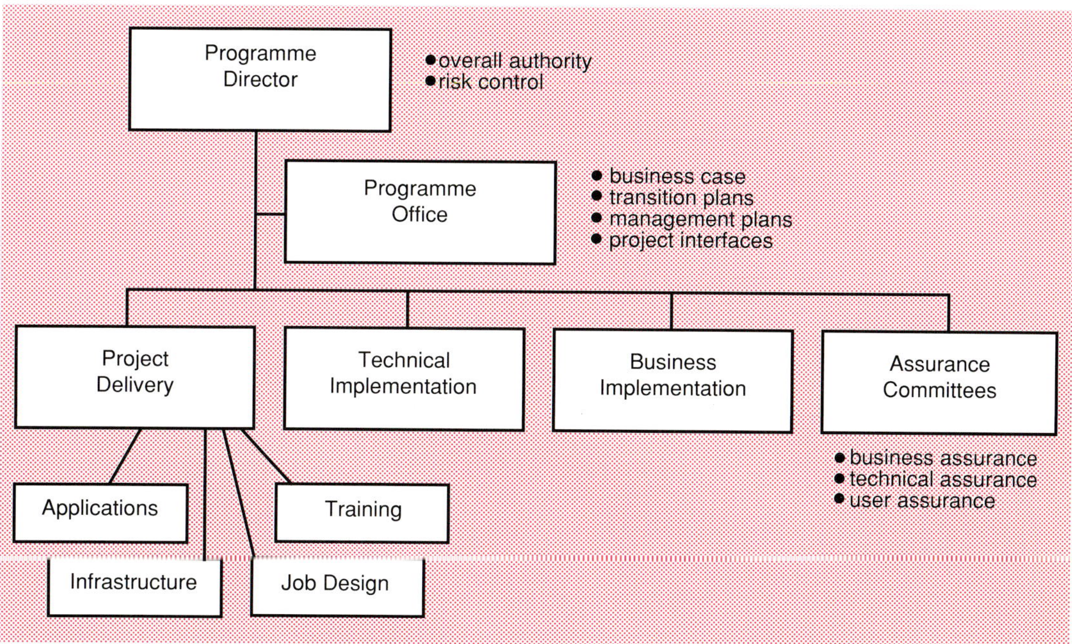

Figure 8.2: Programme and project management organisation

8.5 How was programme management introduced?

Programme management was introduced to provide a management interface between individual projects and the Agency's senior management (see Figure 8.2).

The key aspects were:

- the Programme Director role was fulfilled pro-actively by the Agency's Deputy Chief Executive

- a Programme Office co-ordinated the activity of individual projects

- separate roles were identified for Technical and Business implementation activities due to the scale and diversity of activity.

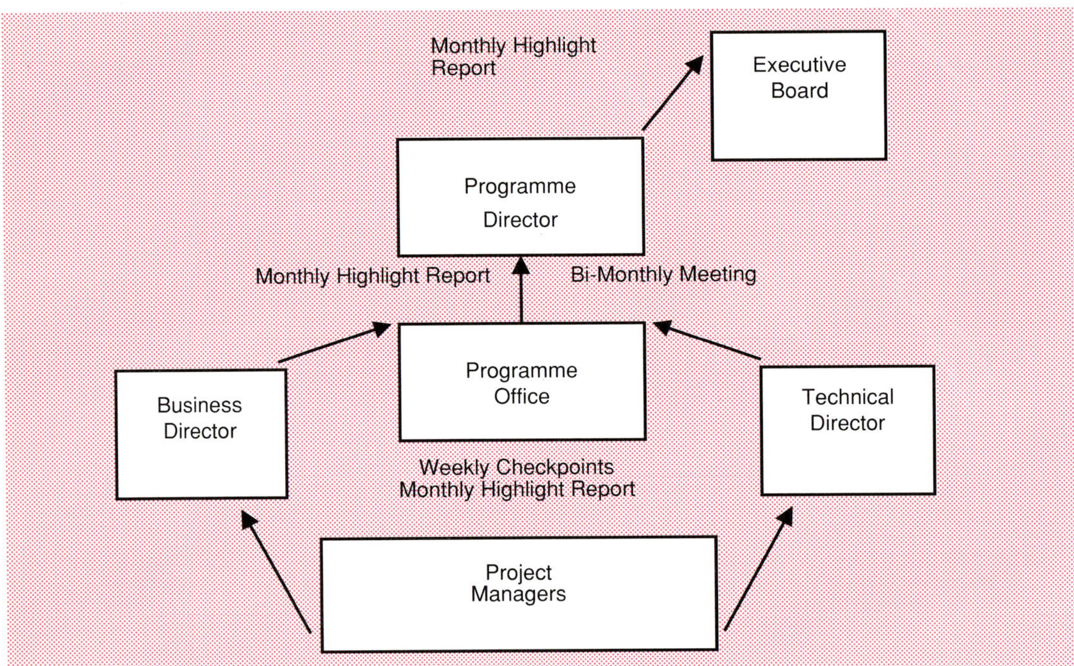

Figure 8.3: Programme management progress reporting

Assurance Committees oversaw the activities of all involved. A programme progress reporting structure was created (see Figure 8.3) which ensured that the right people had the right information at the right time.

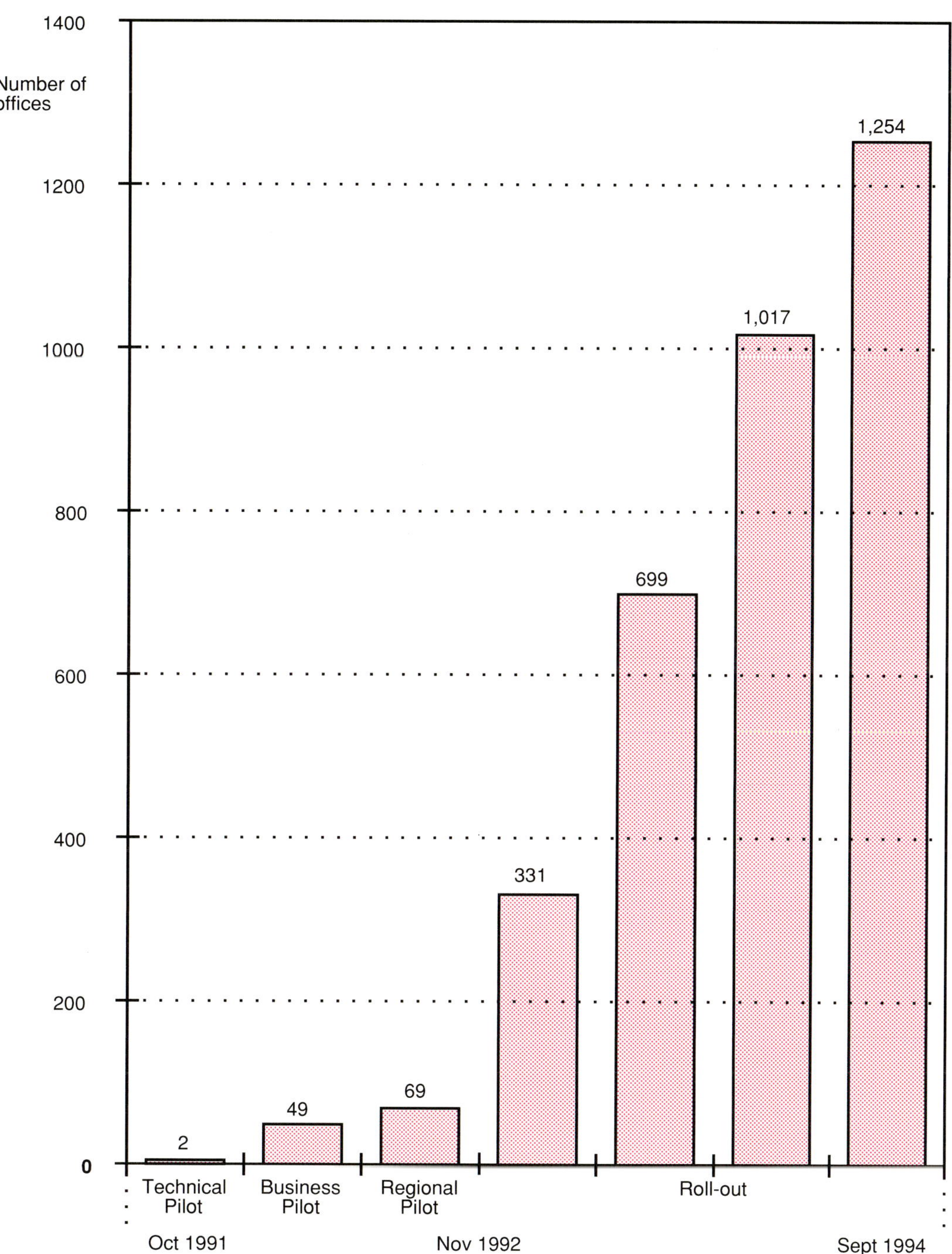

Figure 8.4: The implementation schedule

8.6   Control of change through programme management

The programme management function for the system established an approach to implementation in 'tranches'. This is illustrated in Figure 8.4. It was anticipated that this approach would bring several benefits:

- reduction of technical risk to the programme as a result of the adoption of a medium to long term technical strategy and vision

- optimisation of the implementation approach in the context of the business transformation programme

- effective delivery of the training and change management components of the programme

- more effective management control of the programme through the effective use of stable periods at the end of each tranche for analysis and fine tuning.

The key benefits which were realised as a result of this approach were:

- risks were controlled and minimised

- the anticipated benefits from the programme were quantified and exceeded

- staff morale remained high despite the high levels of change.

The tranched implementation approach within an effective programme and project structure, and an effective programme management organisation have also been critical to the programme's resilience to change.

Several significant areas of change occurred:

- the system was required to handle a doubling of business volumes due to the worsening economic climate

- the programme had to dovetail with a parallel office refurbishment and integration programme

- advances in Information Technology were made during the programme's execution.

The complex relationships between several aspects of the programme that were affected by increased business volumes are illustrated in Figure 8.5.

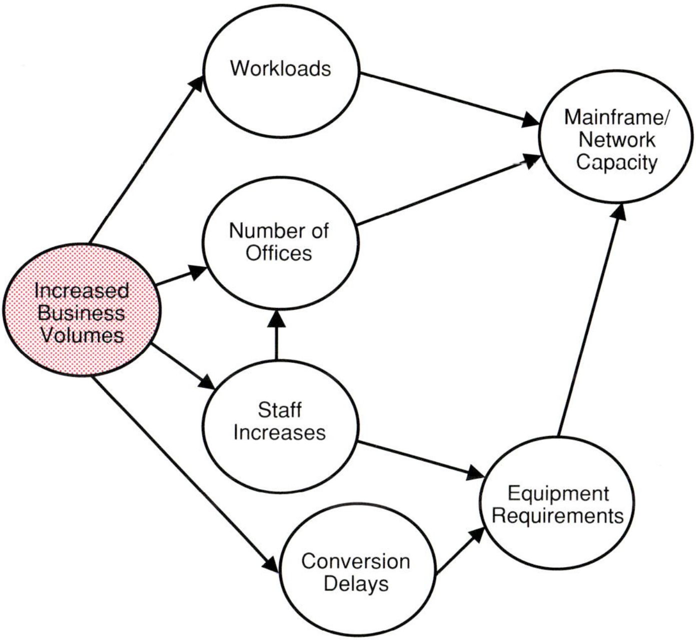

Figure 8.5: The impact of increased business volumes on the programme definition

Increased business volumes

The initial technical and business planning for the programme was based on estimates of business volumes. A thorough understanding of the whole of the programme's architecture enabled effective impact analyses to be performed. The technical architecture was designed with change in mind. When the business volumes increased dramatically, hardware upgrades and fine tuning of the roll out schedule were achieved with comparatively little risk, although significant effort was involved. Effective programme management was instrumental in our management of dynamic changes in business volumes.

Office integration/
refurbishment

The office integration and refurbishment programme meant that the systems programme was hitting a 'moving target'. The topology and exact location of the offices' network were unknown at the outset. Careful planning at a detailed level, with impact analyses for changes, allowed the roll-out to proceed. Frequent communication between the two programmes proved essential.

Advances in
Information
Technology

Inevitably, technology advanced during the course of implementation, both in terms of functionality and performance. The emergence of cost effective Open Systems networks, terminals and servers necessitated the integration of new platforms into a modular initial architecture design (illustrated in Figure 8.6). This, combined with a clear understanding of the relationships and interfaces between all technical components, allowed the Technical Director to introduce increasingly cost competitive Open Systems platforms during the early stages of the programme.

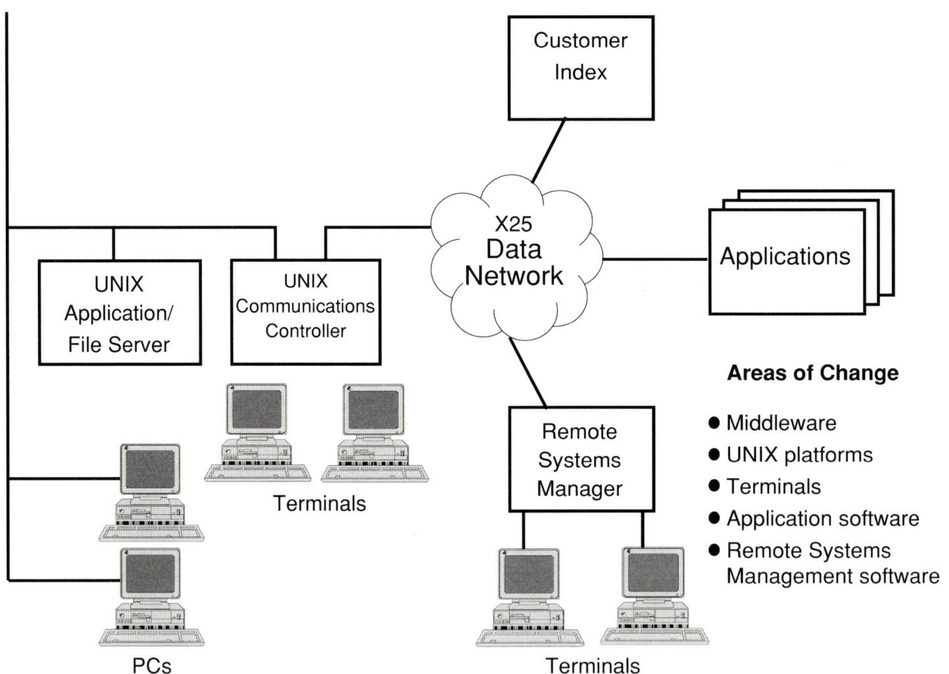

Figure 8.6: New technology

Of course, this involved technology refreshment of the vendors' products and software to manage the network. Integration testing of the end to end product-set allowed the new technology platforms to be introduced during the roll-out at appropriate programme intercept points. Nevertheless, this added significantly to the control aspects of the programme and was only possible through an effective programme management approach.

8.7 Conformance to the CCTA guidance

The key elements of the Agency's approach map well on to the key principles of the CCTA approach as described in *An Introduction to Programme Management*. Namely:

- clear leadership by the business

- active management of all aspects and areas of the programme

- a flexible and responsive framework

- division of the programme into a portfolio of projects.

In some areas of detail the approach deviated from that recommended by CCTA. The key area of difference was the separation of the Business Change Manager into two roles – one business, one technical. This was necessary because of the scale and complexity of the programme, and its changing environment.

8.8 The benefits gained by the business from the programme

The programme has delivered several significant business benefits:

- the delivery of a better service to the public

- significantly increased staff productivity

- increased accuracy and timeliness of customer service

- a flexible platform which enables rather than constrains legislative and other future changes.

**8.9   What might we have
done differently?**

Programme management was undoubtedly the eventual key to success. However, in the early part of the programme, there was no real understanding of the potential benefits of programme management. The programme management processes were followed more by rote than by conviction. In hindsight, if more could have been done to instill the eventual programme management culture earlier in the life of the programme, fewer 'near misses' would have been encountered along the way.

8.10   CCTA commentary

The key success factors in this case study were the use of programme management to maintain the programme schedule over a long time period, and the proper identification of roles in the programme management team, pro-actively led by the senior figure in the organisation.

Although not allocated to identifiable roles such as Business Change Manager, Design Authority and Programme Manager as in the CCTA guidance, the responsibilities were nevertheless specifically undertaken, with similar separation of business and technical responsibilities as in the Business Change Manager and Design Authority roles.

In Figure 8.2 it can be seen that the 'Programme Office' undertook the responsibilities of the Programme Executive members described in the CCTA guidance. Project delivery (the project managers' responsibility), was co-ordinated by the Programme Office – this is the prime responsibility of a Programme Manager in the CCTA guidance. The coherence of the programme's technical implementation (which is the Design Authority's role) was separated from 'business implementation' (for which the Business Change Manager has responsibility, in the CCTA guidance).

In this case study, projects' quality assurance roles (of the Business Assurance Co-ordinator, Technical Assurance Co-ordinator and User Assurance Co-ordinator in PRINCE terms) were performed by Assurance Committees reporting to the Programme Office.

When changes in the scope of the programme came along, the programme management organisation was able to cope.

Annex
Profiles of consultancies

PA Consulting

Profile in outline

PA Consulting Group is an international management and technology consultancy located in 20 countries, with its company headquarters in the UK. PA work with clients in industry, commerce and government to manage complex change and to create business advantage through:

- enhancing strategic thinking

- achieving sustained customer satisfaction

- harnessing the power of technology

- using information effectively

- realising the potential of people

- raising short-term performance.

PA is a centre of excellence for programme and project management and has developed specific implementations of the techniques involved for a large number of public sector organisations and some of Europe's leading businesses.

The case study was produced by Projects Division, Business Transformation Group.

Company name and address

PA Consulting Group
123 Buckingham Palace Road
London SW1W 9SR

Tel: 0171-730 9000
Fax: 0171-333 5050

Touche Ross Management Consultants

Profile in outline

Touche Ross Management Consultants is one of the major management consultancies in the UK, with over 600 professional staff. It is part of Deloitte Touche Tohmatsu International, one of the world's largest accounting and auditing, management consulting and tax services firms with offices in over 116 countries and a staff of 56,000.

As management consultants we appreciate the wide range of issues that arise in managing major change programmes. Our consultants, who have a broad range of experience across a variety of industries and types of programmes, bring a broad business perspective to the problem. Technical experts frequently lose the overall business perspective when working on a large programme. Instead we deploy teams who possess a solid business understanding of the industry balanced with programme management skills appropriate to the client's needs.

Company name and address

Touche Ross Management Consultants
Friary Court
66 Crutched Friars
London EC3N 2NP

Tel: 0171-936 3000
Fax: 0171-480 6958
Telex: 884257 TRFRC G

Ernst & Young

Profile in outline

Ernst & Young provides a full range of management consultancy services. It is an international organisation which has taken a lead in investing in new approaches and methods for tackling current business issues. Its main focus is Performance Improvement and Innovation (including business process improvement) and Information Systems. Working with clients in multi-disciplinary teams is our preferred approach, bringing to bear the broad range of expertise usually necessary to tackle today's management problems.

Ernst & Young provides quality consulting to a wide range of clients in the UK public sector. This covers all aspects of business and IS and embraces implementation and management of change. We retain a strategic and management focus through our services in IS strategy, programme and project management and performance improvement. This is backed by technical specialists in technology, methods, security and audit. Our programme management services include strategy and scoping, planning and management of programmes and the provision of programme management offices.

We bring to bear a wide range of experience in the management of large scale and international change programmes, frequently incorporating significant business reengineering and implementation of IT.

Company name and address

Ernst and Young Management Consultants
Becket House
1 Lambeth Palace Road
London SE1 7EU

Tel: 0171-928 2000
Fax: 0171-928 1345

CSC Computer Sciences Ltd

Profile in outline

Computer Sciences Corporation is the world's largest independent professional services organisation in the computer industry. The company employs 28,500 people worldwide, of whom over 2,000 are based in the UK. Its revenues are divided equally between public sector and commercial markets. CSC is a leader in business re-engineering, information technology consultancy, programme management, project management, systems development and integration.

CSC has worked with a number of companies through the whole range of programme management activities. These include set-up and definition of programmes, activities associated with programme control, setting up and running the programme office and its associated infrastructure and managing the resultant programme benefits.

CSC has worked in programmes with many leading public and private sector clients on both sides of the Atlantic including government, utilities, retail, manufacturing and financial sector organisations.

Within the public sector, CSC has provided programme management support, set up programme offices and programme architectures and provided key individuals to staff the programme management team. We have shadowed programme directors, implemented control tools and techniques and established a programme management culture within a number of client organisations.

Company name and address

CSC Computer Sciences Ltd
279 Farnborough Road
Farnborough
Hampshire GU14 7LS
Tel: 0252-363000
Fax: 0252-370222

IBM

Profile in outline	Programme management in IBM has evolved over many years through experience on many programmes. The company offers the skills, experience and management methodology to successfully design, develop and implement solutions to meet the demanding requirements of government departments. It has wide experience in programme management both in government and in the public utility companies. The company is currently active in large programmes in both government and public utilities.
	IBM can offer to take full responsibility for a programme or provide the consultancy and training for a customer to create their own programme management environment. Services can be tailored to meet the individual needs of each programme.
Company name and address	IBM United Kingdom Ltd Bedfont Lakes 1 New Square Feltham Middlesex TW14 8HB Tel: 0181-818 4000 Fax: 0181-818 5499

Andersen Consulting

Profile in outline

Andersen Consulting is the world's largest management consultancy in the business integration and systems integration field. The firm provides a full range of services to clients from strategic advice to detailed technical assistance. Specialist groups focus on particular sectors. In the UK the firm has a group of over 250 government experts with experience varying from policy through to systems implementation. Andersen Consulting has been involved in many of the UK's largest change programmes and technology.

Company name and address:

Andersen Consulting
2 Arundel Street
London WC2R 3LT

Tel: 0171-438 5000
Fax: 0171-831 1133
Telex: 8812711

Bibliography

A range of publications is available which complement the guidance given in this volume:

Programme Management

A briefing pamphlet is available from the Library, CCTA, Rosebery Court, St Andrew's Business Park, NORWICH, NR7 0HS:

- Managing Programmes of Large-Scale Change

Programme and Project Management Library volumes, which outline the general concepts of the approach to programme management described in detail in this guide and are available from HMSO through its bookshops and agents or by mail order from HMSO Publications Centre, PO Box 276, London SW8 5DT:

- An Introduction to Programme Management
  ISBN: 0 11 330611 3

- A Guide to Programme Management
  ISBN: 0 11 330600 8

PRINCE

The PRINCE Reference Manuals (a boxed set of five Guides) is published by NCC Blackwell and is available from NCC Ltd, Sales Administration (Publications), Oxford Road, Manchester M1 7ED:

- PRINCE Reference Manuals
  ISBN: 1 85554 012 6

A volume of CCTA's Programme and Project Management Library gives an introduction to PRINCE and is published by HMSO and available through its bookshops and agents or by mail order from HMSO Publications Centre, PO Box 276, London SW8 5DT:

- PRINCE – An Outline
  ISBN: 0 11 330599 0

Other

There is a CCTA booklet discussing the role of IS/IT in Business Process Re-engineering, indicating how elements of BPR can be selected to match how far an organisation wishes to go in changing the way it does things. It is published by HMSO and available through its bookshops and agents or by mail order from HMSO Publications Centre, PO Box 276, London SW8 5DT:

- Business Process Re-engineering in the Public Sector
  ISBN: 0 11 330651 2

Glossary

benefits

The enhanced efficiency, economy and effectiveness of future business operations to be delivered by a programme.

benefits management

A formal process within programme management for planning, managing, delivering and measuring the set of benefits which the programme is to provide.

Benefits Realisation phase

The fourth phase of the programme management approach, occurring at the end of each tranche of a programme, and particularly at the end of the full programme. The objectives are to assess operational performance levels against targets in the benefits framework and *blueprint*; to compensate for any short-fall in achievement; to seek additional areas of benefit from the exploitation of the delivered facilities; to ensure lessons learnt are fed into the replanning of the next tranche; and finally, to close down a completed programme (or programme tranche), and ensure that the lessons learnt are fed back into strategy reviews and into future programmes.

blueprint

The section of the Programme Definition Statement which sets out the vision for the programme. The *blueprint* will include business models, operational performance measures, organisation, information systems and support service requirements.

business area

A general term used in the CCTA guidance to refer to that part of an organisation containing the business operations affected by the programme. Business areas may or may not coincide with current organisational units. A business area may cover all the operations of a small organisation, but in a larger organisation it may be preferable to identify and manage change in several business areas separately.

business assurance co-ordination, Business Assurance Co-ordinator (BAC)

The responsibility of planning, monitoring and reporting on a project's business assurance aspects (costs, elapsed time and business case viability). (Carried out by the Business Assurance Co-ordinator (BAC), within the Project Assurance Team (PAT) of a PRINCE project.)

business case

The section of the Programme Definition Statement which provides the justification for the commitment of resources to a programme. The business case should demonstrate that the most cost-effective combination of projects has been selected when compared with costed alternatives. It also provides the wider context and justification for infrastructure investment and the costs of implementing policies and standards.

Business Change Manager (BCM)

A role in the Programme Executive. The BCM is responsible for maximising the improvement to business operations through benefits management, for drawing up the programme's business case, for transition planning and the management of change, and for the management of risk.

business operations

Groupings of one or more business processes which combine to achieve a primary goal of the organisation (for example, assessment and payment of a type of social security benefit).

communications plan

The plan for how the objectives, plans and progress of the programme are to be communicated to staff, to promote a feeling of common ownership, to facilitate knowledge transfer and training, and to ensure that those involved and affected have a common set of expectations throughout the life of the programme.

Design Authority

A role within the Programme Executive, with the responsibility to manage the design of the business and information systems that are affected or created by the programme, ensuring that designs are consistent across all projects in the portfolio and with supporting services and infrastructure designs and plans, and that designs comply with the policies and standards of the organisation and the programme. The Design Authority is also responsible for change control to technical specifications and technical infrastructure.

feasibility study

During the Programme Definition phase, the programme feasibility study is conducted to develop in further detail the business requirements and benefits analysis contained in the Programme Brief – in order to draw up the *blueprint* of the future business operations – and to scope and structure implementation options.

infrastructure

In this guide, infrastructure is broadly defined to include both 'traditional' forms of infrastructure such as IS/IT, telecommunications and estates, as well as supporting services such as accountancy, staffing and personnel.

'Island of Stability'

A review point at the end of a tranche (and overlapping the next tranche) when the programme management team review progress and re-assess benefits, risk and remaining uncertainty, and plan the next tranche in detail.

phase

A part of the programme life cycle, into which activities to manage the programme are grouped. The four phases of Programme Identification, Programme Definition, Programme Execution and Benefits Realisation are defined in this guide. All four phases may be repeated for each tranche of a programme if necessary.

portfolio of projects

See project portfolio.

PRINCE

Projects **In** Controlled Environments, the standard methodology used for project management in government.

programme

A portfolio of projects selected and planned in a co-ordinated way so as to achieve a set of defined business objectives, giving effect to various (and often overlapping) initiatives and/or implementing a strategy. Alternatively, a single, large or very complex project, or a set of otherwise unrelated projects bounded by a business cycle. The programme includes the controlled environment of management responsibilities, activities, documentation and monitoring arrangements by which the portfolio of projects achieve their goals and the broader goals of the programme.

Programme Benefits Review (PBR)

A review to assess achievement of targets and to measure performance levels in the resulting business operations. A PBR also analyses successes and failures in the programme management process. The review is undertaken by a team commissioned by the Programme Director.

Programme Benefits Review (PBR) Report

A report drawn up at the end of the programme (and of each tranche of the programme), describing the findings, conclusions and recommendations of the PBR.

Programme Brief

An output of the Programme Identification phase, describing the programme and giving the terms of reference for the work to be carried out, and the Programme Director's terms of reference.

Programme Definition phase

The second phase of programme management. A feasibility study is carried out to explore options for realising the benefits framework described in the Programme Brief. The programme is fully defined, a benefits management regime established, and funding approval for major projects is obtained. Initial Project Briefs are written, specifying project deliverables and outline project plans. The results of the phase are documented in a Programme Definition Statement.

Programme Definition Statement (PDS)

The agreed statement of objectives and plans between the target business operation, the Programme Director, and the senior management group (Management Board, steering committee) to whom the Programme Director is reporting. The PDS forms the basis for funding the programme and is the key monitoring and control document. It is a dynamic document, maintained throughout the life of the programme.

Programme Director

The senior manager with individual responsibility for the overall success of the programme, and drawn from the management of the target business area. The Programme Executive and the programme's Project Board chairmen formally report to and receive direction from the Programme Director.

Programme Execution phase

The third phase of programme management, in which the project portfolio management and transition activities are undertaken. Compliance with the programme design, corporate and programme policies, standards, and infrastructure plans is monitored and assured.

Programme Executive

The Programme Executive is the group of individuals, supporting the Programme Director, who haves day-to-day management responsibility for the whole programme. The Programme Executive consists of those responsible for the following roles: the Business Change Manager, the Programme Manager, the programme Design Authority. If a Programme Support Office has been established, its head may also attend regular meetings of the Programme Executive.

Programme Identification phase

The first phase of programme management, in which all high-level change proposals from available strategies and initiatives are considered collectively and their objectives and directions translated into one or more achievable programmes of work. For each programme identified a Programme Brief is written and a Programme Director appointed.

programme management

The selection and co-ordinated planning of a portfolio of projects so as to achieve a set of defined business objectives, and the efficient execution of these projects within a controlled environment such that they realise maximum benefit for the resulting business operations.

Programme Manager

The individual responsible for the day-to-day management of the programme on behalf of the Programme Director. The Programme Manager is a member of the Programme Executive.

programme plan

A collective term for the benefits management plan, risk management plan, transition plan, project portfolio plan and design management plan, which are components of the Programme Definition Statement.

Programme Support Office (PSO)

An organisation giving administrative assistance to the Programme Manager and the Programme Executive, particularly with management information reporting. The PSO may, where appropriate, serve both the programme and the individual projects.

Project Board

The executive organisation which provides overall direction and guidance to a PRINCE managed project. All Project Boards within a programme report to the Programme Director.

Project Brief

A product of the Programme Definition phase which contains an outline specification for a project within the programme plan.

project portfolio

The constituent projects within a programme, which will deliver the products needed to move the business forward from the current business operations to those described in the *blueprint*.

technical assurance co-ordination, Technical Assurance Co-ordinator (TAC)_

The responsibility of planning, monitoring and reporting on the technical integrity of a project's products. (Carried out by the Technical Assurance Co-ordinator (TAC), within the Project Assurance Team (PAT) of a PRINCE project.)

tranche

A block of work within the programme, identified to facilitate the programme's management.

transition plan

A component of a Programme Definition Statement, describing how the transition from the current business operation to the new environment of the *blueprint* is to be managed.